The Demography of Sociopolitical Conflict in Japan, 1721–1846

INSTITUTE OF EAST ASIAN STUDIES
UNIVERSITY OF CALIFORNIA • BERKELEY
CENTER FOR JAPANESE STUDIES

The Demography of Sociopolitical Conflict in Japan, 1721–1846

JAMES W. WHITE

A publication of the Institute of East Asian Studies, University of California, Berkeley. Although the Institute is responsible for the selection and acceptance of manuscripts in this series, responsibility for the opinions expressed and for the accuracy of statements rests with their authors.

The Japan Research Monograph series is one of several publications series sponsored by the Institute of East Asian Studies in conjunction with its constituent units. The others include the China Research Monograph series, the Korea Research Monograph series, the Indochina Research Monograph series, and the Research Papers and Policy Studies series. A list of recent publications appears at the back of the book.

Correspondence may be sent to:
Ms. Joanne Sandstrom, Managing Editor
Institute of East Asian Studies
University of California
Berkeley, California 94720

The author acknowledges with gratitude the generous permission of Yoshikawa Kōbunkan publishers to reprint the material in Table 1 from its publication, Minami Kazuo's *Bakumatsu Edo Shakai no Kenkyū,* and of Shibundō publishers to reprint the material in Table 2 from its publication, Sekiyama Naotarō's *Nihon no Jinkō.*

Contents

ONE

Introduction

The relationship between population and conflict has occupied both scholars and public officials since time immemorial. Teeming masses, climbing birthrates, floods of migrants, food supplies insufficient for the mouths they must feed, and high concentrations of rambunctious young males have seemed in many times and places to foreshadow conflict, either domestic or international. But factors behind these "shadows" have seldom been deeply penetrated by observers, and the implications drawn from systematic, scholarly studies have been in many ways mutually contradictory.

It is not my purpose to clarify all the implications for human conflict of demographic states and changes, but merely to examine a few aspects of the topic in such a way that modest generalization may be possible. Specifically, I wish here to disaggregate the topic of population and examine the relationships of its several dimensions to social conflict and political protest in one preindustrial agrarian society: Japan in the eighteenth and nineteenth centuries, under the rule of the Tokugawa shōguns. The dimensions of population that I shall examine are absolute size, density, pressure (on the food supply), distribution, and crisis (resulting from natural calamity), and changes in all of these.[1] Conflict will also be disaggregated; my focus is on conflict internal to Japanese society only and, within that society, on the contentious behavior of the common people in Japan's 73 provinces.[2] This behavior includes legal petition and litigation directed at other commoners or at the authorities; social conflict between individual commoners or between groups of

The research on which this essay is based was supported by the National Science Foundation (SES-8308413), the Social Science Research Council, the Fulbright Commission, the Carolina Population Center, and the University of North Carolina University Research Council, whose generous assistance is acknowledged with gratitude. Moreover, I have profited from the helpful comments of Jack Goldstone, Hayami Akira, Ron Rindfuss, and Saitō Osamu. However, all opinions, conclusions, and errors herein are the responsibility of the author and not the above groups or individuals.

them; social conflict that eventuated in overtures to the government for adjudication or relief or otherwise drew officialdom in; and pure protest action opposed to government policy, performance, or incumbents.

Each of the above elements will be described in detail below, as will the data to be used to address the questions before us. But rather than jump into the data, I shall first review some of the relationships found by other scholars, focusing on other eras and cultures, in order that we might have a better idea of what to expect to find in Tokugawa Japan.

Size

Other things being equal, one would expect to find more conflict of all kinds in, say, China or India than in Japan or the Trobriand Islands. As the number of individuals in a society increases, the number of social relationships grows geometrically, and so do the opportunities for conflict. For this reason, we are interested here in magnitudes and frequencies of conflict per capita, not in the absolute, and in changes in per capita levels of contention that do not simply reflect changes in absolute population size. Population size alone has not been clearly related to forms or frequencies of contention except in the gross sense expressed above (Sanders 1981:16–17, 178ff.; Choucri 1984:ch. 1). Population increase, on the contrary, is arguably associated with disproportionately increased levels of collective behavior (Wolf 1969; Choucri 1974:ch. 11), and it is indirectly associated with conflict through its significant influence on the cast of contenders in a society, the resources at their disposal, and the ability of governments to control them (Tilly et al. 1975). Indeed, according to Jack Goldstone (1988; n.d.), one of the major factors in the political and social upheavals of seventeenth-century Turkey, China, and England was the previous century's population increase, which contributed to inflation and governmental fiscal difficulty, increased competition among the more numerous sons of the elite for elite positions, and new (and largely untaxed) economic pursuits that diminished the government's share of the resources available and indirectly exacerbated conflict when the government tried to extract their fruits from the people.

Goldstone's work, like that of others, implies the significance of population pressure, not simply growth, insofar as it assumes a relatively static agrarian economy and government. Those who have focused on growth per se have often found less impact: Ted Gurr and Herman Weil (1973) found a modest relationship in a sample of modern societies, but such relationships sometimes disappear in multivariate analyses (Zimmermann 1983). And although Douglas Hibbs found some forms of conflict to vary with population growth (1973:28–30), others dispute this finding

(Sanders 1981). With the caveat that pressure rather than pure size (or change therein) may be at work here, one notes that the null findings tend to come from the analysis of modern societies and the positive findings from preindustrial societies like Tokugawa Japan. Thus we might speculate that increasing population, if not larger population, will be associated with higher levels of popular contention in the provinces of early modern Japan.

Density

Population density, like size, gains most of its putative significance in tandem with other factors, like arable land or food supply. In its own right, it is occasionally linked—through the agency of crowded living conditions—to conflict behavior (Choucri 1984:ch. 4; Zimmermann 1983:99), but little more has been found (Choucri 1984:ch. 1). Indeed, there are data from both modern and preindustrial societies (including Japan) that suggest that collective behavior is more common in countries and in regions within countries in which population is less rather than more densely concentrated (Gurr and Weil 1973; Skinner 1987). Crowding we may dismiss—if it contributed unequivocally to conflict, Japan today would be absolutely Hobbesian rather than one of the world's less violent societies. And density per se on a broader scale is probably of negligible account unless manifest as a component of urbanism or pressure on resources.

Population Pressure

Population pressure is the area of primary emphasis in arguments over the relevance of population to conflict. Absolute levels of pressure—usually conceived as the ratio of population to food supply—have been linked repeatedly to contention (Choucri 1974:ch. 11; 1984:ch. 1; Zimmermann 1983:99). Even when density is low, where the proportion of arable land is even lower, pressure—and hypothetically conflict—may be high (Skinner 1987; White 1988). That "conflict arises when growing populations compete for a shrinking resource base" (Murdock 1987) is but the baldest statement of the asserted connection of increasing population pressure to collective behavior (McClintock 1987; Wolf 1969; Zimmermann 1983:99). The findings of Goldstone regarding pressure have been cited above; research in other agrarian societies underscores them (Perry 1980:vii, 2ff.; Kuhn 1980; Midlarsky 1982). Indeed, the entire structure of James Scott's (1976) penetrating analysis of peasant contention is, in Paul Greenough's (1983) view, predicated on rapid population increase and an ensuing "massive land hunger" in twentieth-century Southeast Asia.

Again, however, such a picture must be tempered a bit. Qualitative observations of the pressure-contention link are forced to yield partially in multivariate analyses, which attribute to them a significant, but undramatic and often indirect role (Gurr and Weil 1973), and highlight the necessity of disaggregating the concept—it may not be total pressure but rather the number of unproductive mouths (as shown by the dependency ratio) relative to the food supply that contributes to conflict. Another factor that must be taken into account, in Asia at least, is agricultural involution—it is an open question how much population pressure must increase before people become unable to squeeze any further increment of production out of their land (Choucri 1984:ch. 5). And population pressure entails a theoretical problem: does high or increasing pressure imply high levels of dissatisfaction, frustration, unmet needs, and consequently collective action; or does it imply a paucity of the resources and opportunities people need to protest or contend effectively and thus less conflict? This question in turn goes to the center of one of the most important questions in the area of collective behavior: are deprivation and consequent frustration at the heart of contention, or is rational calculation of ends and means? We shall not focus directly on this question here, but our examination of the relationship between population pressure and conflict may eventually cast some light obliquely upon it.

Despite the caveats offered above, the preponderance of evidence suggests that we should expect to find higher levels of popular contention in those provinces of Tokugawa Japan with higher demographic pressure on the food supply and in those where this pressure is increasing. We should remain aware of contrary possibilities and of the interaction of factors: perhaps sudden increase in pressure (as the result of natural disaster) makes protest a rational alternative to passive starvation. In other words, perhaps pressure is a constant, a precondition that requires a catalytic event in order to become a direct cause of conflict. But provisionally we shall accord it an independent role.

Distribution

The distribution of populations may be structural or physical. Structural distribution includes ratios of men to women, young to old, and dependent to productive—all of which have been associated with conflict, but none of which is amenable to analysis with the data available to us. We shall therefore dwell longer on physical distribution, specifically, urbanization and migration.

For much of human history cities have been regarded both as centers of innovation, wealth, and culture, and as cesspools of the deprived, depraved, criminal, and insurrectionary. Recent research has put generalizations of the latter type in serious question (Cornelius 1970, 1975; White 1973; Parvin 1973); however, if one can avoid linking the putative qualities of urbanites to conflict, there is unquestionably a tie: greater concentrations of people facilitate communication (including communication of grievances); imply greater concentration of social, economic, and political resources of all sorts and greater proximity of political targets to the people; and facilitate mobilization of large numbers of people for any purpose, including contention (Tilly 1968, 1978; Dahl and Tufte 1973; Moore 1978; Bohstedt 1983). And indeed, the very existence of cities seems to breed higher levels and distinctive repertoires of conflict. The exact strength of the relationship is a matter of strenuous debate (Huntington 1968; Gurr 1980:186; Hibbs 1973; Sanders 1981:16; Choucri 1984:ch. 4), although the characteristic urban locus of certain forms of contention in preindustrial societies, such as the food riot, is not.

Unsurprisingly, those who suggest a link between cities and conflict suggest also a link between more, bigger, and growing cities and more conflict. Over long periods this linkage appears to be valid (Zimmermann 1983; Goldstone n.d.), especially in societies in which there is not already a well-developed urban context (Gurr and Weil 1973). But if urban growth is very rapid, it appears to depress levels of conflict: floods of urban migrants apparently require some time to become acquainted with new environments and new fellow urbanites before they can act in any meaningful way collectively (White 1973; Cornelius 1970, 1975; Tilly et al. 1975). This observation flies in the face of the conventional wisdom concerning urban conflict in Tokugawa Japan, which presumes that cityward migrants were significant sources of unrest, but it is well documented in other societies and may empirically hold in Japan as well.

Indeed, unless Japan is sui generis, we should not expect to find (a) that urban unrest varies directly with migrant inflow or that (b) migrants are overrepresented in urban contention. In actuality, urbanism in Tokugawa Japan did not change radically during the period for which we have population data. Consequently, we shall look closely at periods of famine (when refugees streamed into some cities), but otherwise expect the hypothetical statements about slow change in urbanism over time to be more relevant than those about rapid change. Aside from certain forms of conflict concentrated in urban areas, perhaps we should not even expect to find strong relationships between degree of urbanization and magnitude of conflict. The argument may be made that it is in the less urban areas along the peripheries of Japan's different regions that we shall find more conflict—that the sparseness of population here is matched or even surpassed by the sparseness of governmental presence, thus enhancing the opportunities for effective collective action (Skinner 1987; White 1988a).

Thus urbanization as a process shall not occupy us much here, although urbanism as a state or level will, as will the new urbanites themselves—this attention, however, derives more from their putative role in urban contention than from any theoretical basis. Once we look beyond rates of urbanization, we might well expect to find that Tokugawa Japan's more urban regions are characterized by higher levels of conflict and by distinctive forms of conflict as well. Such expectations do not rely on any presumption of urbanites' dissatisfactions—indeed, most evidence suggests that city dwellers are, if anything, more satisfied than rural (Cornelius 1970, 1975)—but rather on the characteristics of cities noted above. We expect that it is the context, not the psyche, of the townsman that explains his obstreperous behavior.

Crisis

As several comments above suggest, the sorts of rapid changes in population size, pressure, and distribution brought about by famine, epidemic, and natural disaster—especially in preindustrial societies like Tokugawa Japan—have been associated with collective behavior of different types. The relevance of natural disaster could be conceptualized in terms of dashed hopes, public relief that is not forthcoming, frustration, or immiseration; for our purposes it is best thought of demographically: increased pressure due to sudden reduction of the food supply and increased flows of migrant refugees. It is possible, of course, that any linkages between disaster and contention that do exist work through other agencies than population change, but the demographic implications of famine, for example, are so salient that one is well advised to attend to them also.

The argument that dearth is tied to conflict is an old one. Ted Gurr (1968, 1970), James Davies (1971), and Crane Brinton (1965) are simply some of the better-known proponents of the view that absolute or relative deprivation, either individual or collective, especially when sudden, drastic, following a period of improvement, or unaccompanied by downward revision of expectations, leads directly or indirectly to increased levels of contention in society (see also Muller 1979:135). As is the case with other aspects of demographic change discussed above, disaster-induced population pressure does not act in a vacuum: contextual factors such as relief, tax cuts, repression, or the opportunity for out-migration can weaken the link to conflict. If no conceivable avenue of respite is visible, then contention is unlikely; and if famine becomes acute enough, physical incapacity may obviate any action whatsoever. But recent research (Tong 1985; Shingles 1987) has refined the relationship and suggests that if dearth and deprivation are politicized and people find the cost of collective action to be acceptably low (especially when calculated as the ratio of potential participants to government coercive capabilities) and its benefit to be sufficiently high (e.g., survival instead of starvation or bankruptcy), then the connection is much stronger than simpler analyses linking deprivation and contention would suggest (Barnes and Kaase 1979).[3]

In the case of Tokugawa Japan, the research described above suggests an effect from demographic crisis on conflict. Many segments of the population lived rather close to the subsistence level, and even if they got along reasonably well in normal times, their margin was small, making sudden deprivation an endemic threat. Nonagrarian populations, in both country and city, were crucially vulnerable to interruptions in the flow of foodstuffs regardless of standard of living. Natural disasters, including highly localized ones, are inevitable in preindustrial society, especially in a feudal society wherein one relatively autonomous domain might or might not supply a needy neighbor. Japan's isolation from international commerce meant that imported food was not a possibility. Deprivation was commonly politicized, or at least "socialized" rather than atomized: if the common people did not look to the government for relief, they certainly turned to their betters within the commoner class rather than lapsing into individualistic desperation or torpor. The government, for its part, was as likely to exacerbate (and further politicize) calamities as to ameliorate them: it seldom willingly reduced its own extractions from the people just because they were suffering. And finally, this rapacious inclination was not matched by coercive capabilities, which were throughout the Tokugawa era unimpressive in operation and increasingly so: draconian laws were enforced and sanguinary punishments imposed but with extraordinary and growing inconsistency (White 1988c). Any reasonably thoughtful peasant could quite easily come to the conclusion that collective remonstration against government inflexibility in the face of crop failure was an eminently rational path to take (White 1988b; 1988d). Thus our expectation, as we move toward a closer look at population and conflict, is that demographic crises of all kinds should be linked with contentious behavior.

TWO

Demography and Dissidence in Tokugawa Japan

The population of Japan during the Tokugawa era (1600–1868) went through three stages: rapid growth during the seventeenth century, extraordinary stability during the eighteenth, and the beginnings of increase again during the nineteenth. Estimates of the national population in 1600 range from 6 to 20 million (Taeuber 1958; Hanley and Yamamura 1977; Sekiyama 1959), with 12 million probably the most accurate (Nishikawa 1985:30ff.). In 1721 the central government of the shōgun ordered the first of a series of censuses, which indicated a population of 26,065,425 (although Kitō Hiroshi's [1983b:12] estimate for 1721 is already 31 million, indicating growth during the seventeenth century of some 150 percent; see also Hayami 1988). Data for eighteen subsequent censuses have survived, as shown in Table 1, and depict both the stability of the eighteenth century and the recovery of the nineteenth. The period between 1732 and 1744 includes the Kyōhō famine; the 1780s, the Temmei famine; and the 1830s, the Tempō famine, three of the four greatest famines of the era.[1] For the most part, however, the nineteenth century figures represent growth.

By the end of the Tokugawa era, the national population had grown to well over 30 million; in 1877 it was 36 million (Kitō 1983b:12; Nishikawa 1985:30ff.). The apparent growth thus represented is to some extent spurious. The Tokugawa censuses were incomplete: they included only the commoner population (the samurai aristocracy accounted for between 5 and 10 percent of the population) and perhaps only the rural commoner population (the cities probably accounted for another 10 percent); moreover, documentation was far from exhaustive (Hanley and Yamamura 1977; Jansen and Rozman 1986; Sekiyama 1959:114; Saitō 1988). Thus the censuses omitted somewhere in the vicinity of 5 million people, and the most accurate estimate of the national population between the late seventeenth century and the early nineteenth is probably Hayami Akira's 31 million (Nishikawa 1985:30ff.). But the trends

Table 1
The Population of Japan, 1721–1846

Year	Population	Index (1721=100)
1721	26,065,425	100.0
1726	26,548,998	101.9
1732	26,921,816	103.3
1744	26,153,450	100.3
1750	25,917,830	99.4
1756	26,070,712	100.1
1762	25,921,458	99.5
1768	26,252,057	100.7
1774	25,990,451	99.7
1780	26,010,600	99.8
1786	25,086,466	96.2
1792	24,891,441	95.5
1798	25,471,033	97.7
1804	25,621,957	98.3
1822	26,602,110	102.1
1828	27,201,400	104.4
1834	27,063,907	103.8
1840	25,918,412	99.4
1846	26,907,625	103.2

SOURCE: Minami 1978:180.

noted above—growth, stability, recovery—are undisputed and corroborated by data on the growth rate in the number of villages nationwide (Kitō 1983b; Umemura 1965). Moreover, we may assume here that whatever biases were at work were consistent over time and across provinces (Jansen and Rozman 1986:286). Therefore, although we cannot compare the census data with either the 12 million estimate of 1600 or the official figure of 1877, we can compare the censuses with one another in order to analyze the population between 1721 and 1846.

Population: Macrostability, Mesovariety, Microdynamism

Given the period we are able to examine, the picture presented in Table 1 is consistent with the common assertion that Japan's population was largely unchanged during the latter part of the Tokugawa era. Various explanations have been offered for this stasis: famine, epidemic, natural disaster, purposive population control, diminishing completeness of the censuses, and the achievement of a stable balance between population, technology, and land in a mature agrarian society (Jannetta 1987; Smith 1977; Hanley and Yamamura 1977; Sekiyama 1959; Taeuber 1958; Kitō 1983b). My concern here is not to explain this phenomenon, but to use population to explain other phenomena. First, however, we should see if this national-level picture is in fact accurate, that is, if Japan's population did indeed remain so stable throughout the era.

Regional Variations

A look at our census data region by region and province by province indicates that the national picture obscures a great deal of change. Regionally (see Table 2 and Figure 1), we can see three major trends: first, stagnation in the far northern Tōhoku region, noted for its precarious agricultural situation, rugged topography and harsh climate, and frequent crop failures. Second, stagnation also in the Kantō and the Kinki, home respectively to the major cities of Edo and Ōsaka. Third, a pattern of overall growth elsewhere in the country: nine census-to-census comparisons can be made in each of the seven remaining regions, and of these 63 comparisons, only ten are decreases. Of the ten, two occurred from 1756 to 1786 (the period that included the Temmei famine) and six from 1834 to 1846, the period of the Tempō famine. Where not held in check by natural factors (whether endemic, as in the Tōhoku, or occasional, as elsewhere) or by the nature of Tokugawa urbanism (discussed below), then, Japan's population evinces growth tendencies throughout the period quite at odds with the macro-level picture (Hayami 1988:188–189). Indeed, in southern Japan even poor-crop years saw population growth (Kitō 1985). And in fact even these regional figures indicate that unmitigated stagnation was true only of the Kinki: the Kantō's population was at a 100-year high by 1846 (this despite the Tempō famine), and the Tōhoku appears to have begun to grow in the early nineteenth century only to be set back by the same famine.

Province-level data are similarly variable, with decreases offsetting increases until the nineteenth century (see Table 3). Within the Tōhoku, only Mutsu province declined; Dewa, on the Japan Sea side of the region, was slightly larger in 1846 than in 1721. In the Kantō, population shrank everywhere except in the most distant province, Awa; in the Kinki, however, depopulation only occurred in the core of the region (Ōsaka was located in Settsu, and the city of Kyōto in Yamashiro), while peripheral Tamba, Tango, Tajima, and Awaji at least held their own, and Kii nearly did. Outside of these regions, only four provinces suffered absolute decreases between 1721 and 1846: Echizen and Wakasa on the Japan Sea (which may have been near enough to the cities of the Kinki

Table 2

Regional Population Variation, 1721–1846

	1721	1750	1756	1786	1798	1804	1822	1828	1834	1846
Kinki	100.0	95.3	97.7	94.7	93.5	92.9	96.0	97.0	95.7	93.5
Tokai	100.0	102.0	100.6	99.2	100.1	100.6	107.1	106.4	106.3	106.6
Kantō	100.0	98.5	97.9	85.4	85.0	83.8	82.8	84.8	81.4	86.6
Tōhoku	100.0	94.4	92.1	83.4	86.0	87.1	89.0	92.4	92.7	88.7
Tozan	100.0	100.3	102.8	104.1	106.1	106.0	110.0	118.2	114.3	110.1
Hokuriku	100.0	100.2	102.6	97.8	105.3	107.0	111.9	120.5	122.6	117.6
San'in	100.0	105.1	109.2	112.0	118.8	120.0	127.3	129.9	132.7	124.8
San'yo	100.0	100.7	102.4	105.4	106.8	109.9	111.2	119.8	121.8	120.2
Shikoku	100.0	102.0	104.9	108.4	111.7	114.9	122.3	123.8	126.1	126.8
Kyūshū	100.0	102.9	104.5	104.9	105.3	107.3	110.4	111.3	112.2	113.8

NOTE: For constituent provinces, see Figure 1.
SOURCE: Sekiyama 1959:82–83.

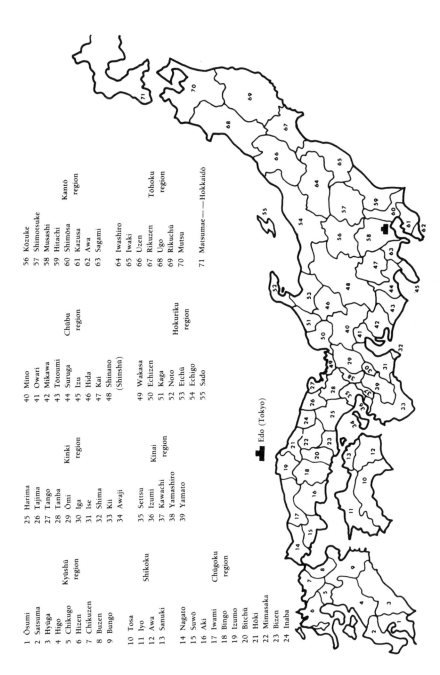

1 Osumi
2 Satsuma
3 Hyūga
4 Higo
5 Chikugo
6 Hizen — Kyūshū region
7 Chikuzen
8 Buzen
9 Bungo

10 Tosa
11 Iyo — Shikoku
12 Awa
13 Sanuki

14 Nagato
15 Suwō
16 Aki
17 Iwami
18 Bingo
19 Izumo — Chūgoku region
20 Bitchū
21 Hōki
22 Mimasaka
23 Bizen
24 Inaba

25 Harima
26 Tajima
27 Tango
28 Tanba
29 Ōmi — Kinki region
30 Iga
31 Ise
32 Shima
33 Kii
34 Awaji

35 Settsu
36 Izumi — Kinai region
37 Kawachi
38 Yamashiro
39 Yamato

40 Mino
41 Owari
42 Mikawa
43 Totoumi
44 Suruga — Chūbu region
45 Izu
46 Hida
47 Kai
48 Shinano (Shinshū)

49 Wakasa
50 Echizen
51 Kaga
52 Noto — Hokuriku region
53 Etchū
54 Echigo
55 Sado

56 Kōzuke
57 Shimotsuke
58 Musashi
59 Hitachi
60 Shimōsa — Kantō region
61 Kazusa
62 Awa
63 Sagami

64 Iwashiro
65 Uzen
66 Iwaki
67 Rikuzen — Tohoku region
68 Ugo
69 Rikuchū
70 Mutsu

71 Matsumae — Hokkaidō

Edo (Tokyo)

Figure 1. Japan and its provinces in the Tokugawa period

Table 3

Variation in Population and Total Conflict, by Province

Province	Population			Total Conflict		
	1721	1798	1846	1700–1740	1780–1820	1825–1865
Mutsu*	100	81	82	100	200	267
Dewa**	100	97	103	100	350	550
Musashi	100	88	94	100	188	288
Sagami	100	90	97	100	700	867
Kōzuke	100	89	75	100	1000	1300
Shimotsuke	100	73	68	100	300	1050
Hitachi	100	69	73	100	500	1100
Kazusa	100	90	88	100	700	1000
Shimoosa	100	89	98	100	240	140
Awa	100	108	117	100	33	100
Echigo	100	113	126	100	440	520
Sado	100	90	100	100	200	155
Etchū	100	110	129	100	160	400
Kaga	100	90	114	100	120	240
Noto	100	113	127	—	100	92
Echizen	100	95	95	100	300	625
Wakasa	100	89	78	100	600	2000
Izu	100	110	120	100	21	433
Suruga	100	100	116	100	450	513
Tōtōmi	100	103	106	100	300	750
Mikawa	100	100	102	100	260	500
Owari	100	111	118	100	100	900
Mino	100	102	105	100	500	825
Hida	100	114	129	100	15	90
Kai	100	107	107	100	600	1200
Shinano	100	107	114	100	300	482
Settsu	100	100	94	100	578	933
Kawachi	100	92	92	100	210	330
Izumi	100	91	91	100	289	311
Yamashiro	100	86	80	—	100	94
Yamato	100	83	88	100	640	160
Ōmi	100	90	90	100	220	360
Ise	100	89	93	100	600	400
Iga	100	80	90	—	100	83
Shima	100	133	133	—	—	—

(continued)

Province	Population			Total Conflict		
	1721	1798	1846	1700–1740	1780–1820	1825–1865
Harima	100	97	94	100	122	244
Awaji	100	91	109	—	100	366
Tamba	100	100	100	100	160	193
Tango	100	115	115	100	92	107
Tajima	100	107	113	100	210	530
Kii	100	90	96	100	550	550
Bizen	100	94	91	100	125	275
Bitchū	100	100	106	100	250	275
Mimasaka	100	84	89	100	46	215
Bingo	100	100	113	100	200	100
Aki	100	136	153	100	150	344
Inaba	100	108	108	100	28	78
Hōki	100	131	138	100	22	19
Oki	100	100	150	—	100	1300
Izumo	100	123	141	100	113	12
Iwami	100	119	114	100	173	180
Nagato	100	119	124	100	267	100
Suō	100	138	169	100	35	88
Sanuki	100	121	130	100	50	550
Awa	100	112	132	100	250	488
Tosa	100	114	131	100	343	129
Iyo	100	106	120	100	450	388
Chikuzen	100	103	117	—	100	30
Chikugo	100	100	111	100	225	225
Hizen	100	110	116	100	62	62
Higo	100	108	125	100	1150	1000
Buzen	100	92	100	100	1100	400
Bungo	100	88	90	100	575	75
Hyūga	100	110	119	100	138	163
Satsuma	100	160	160	—	—	100
Ōsumi	100	109	91	100	300	900
Iki	100	100	150	—	—	—
Tsushima	100	50	100	—	—	—

* Mutsu: Mutsu, Rikuchu, Rikuzen, Iwashiro, and Iwaki provinces.
**Dewa: Ugo and Uzen provinces.

to be drawn into their population-consuming orbits), Ise and Iga on Ise Bay, Bizen and Mimasaka near the Inland Sea, and Bungo and Ōsumi on the southeast periphery of Kyūshū. Additionally, four provinces lost population between 1721 and 1798 but regained it by 1846, and 11 of the 1721–1846 net-loss provinces had at least recovered by 1846 some of the population lost during the eighteenth century. Thus macro-level stagnation (or lack of variation in the demographic variables we hope to relate to conflict) is misleading; on the "meso-level" (region and locality) we can see considerable absolute change and variation in direction of change (see also Hanley and Yamamura 1977; Hayami 1973b, 1978).

As noted, the most salient exceptions to the overall pattern of growth are visible in the Tōhoku and in the most urbanized regions. The Tōhoku enjoyed, during the seventeenth century, considerable population growth, which reversed itself during the eighteenth (Hayami 1982a:78ff.). The explanation seems to be more climatological than political: lords appear less to have pushed their people to a point where stringent self-limitation and vulnerability to crop failure were inevitable than did nature and, as the data suggest, the demographic situation was more one of long-term decline than short-term (Hayami in Jansen and Rozman 1986). But during the eighteenth century, population stability, in a context of rising economic activity, improved real economic production per capita. In the nineteenth century, demographic sparseness meant high capacity for growth, which, combined with a wave of protoindustrialization, led to both economic and demographic growth that continued on into the years following the Tokugawa era (Hayami in Jansen and Rozman 1986; Saitō 1985; Kitō 1983b:69ff., 86ff.). This growth is evident even in some parts of Mutsu province: data available for Yonezawa and Aizu domains indicate that demographic decline bottomed out just before the end of the eighteenth century and was followed thereafter by consistent growth.

The situation in the Kantō and the Kinki was a result of urbanism in early modern Japan: with high death rates and low birth rates (urbanites were disproportionately male), the cities were consumers of people, relying predominantly on in-migration to maintain their size. The more urban regions (and their hinterlands, which supplied them with food and manufactures of all kinds) were also centers of economic activity; hence, both urbanism and level of economic development were during the Tokugawa era negatively related to population growth on the regional level (Hayami 1975:237; Yomiuri Shimbun Sha 1967:195). The effect was regional, not just provincial, because the outlying provinces of the urban regions gave up their population to the cities via migration, and the cities returned little of it to them while still, at best, maintaining themselves (Sasaki 1978). If the economic dynamism of the cities faltered, then lessened flows of in-migrants quickly led to their decline.

We shall return soon to the subject of the city. For the moment, it is sufficient to note three things: local and regional data reveal considerable demographic dynamism; the negative aspects of this dynamism were the long-term effects of northern locale and urbanism (synergistically epitomized in Kōzuke, Shimotsuke, and Hitachi on the northern edge of the Kantō: see, for example, Nagasu 1986); and the population growth that came to characterize more and more of the country during the nineteenth century appears to have been associated with considerable economic growth and—despite the highly unequal distribution of the fruits of this growth—apparently real improvement in the lives of the common people (Smith 1959; Hanley and Yamamura 1977; Hayami 1978 and in Jansen and Rozman 1986; inter al).

This putative improvement was the result of the process of "protoindustrialization," that is, the predominantly rural growth of market-oriented, nonagrarian economic activities (often termed *nōkan yogyō* or "by-employments") within an agriculturally commercializing but as yet nonindustrial context (Saitō 1985; Mendels 1982). This process, to which we shall return repeatedly below, was so widespread from the early eighteenth century onward that in many villages the actual bulk of the villagers' incomes came from such—largely untaxed—sources. It was also of considerable social and demographic significance. Socially (this subject is treated in detail in White 1989), protoindustrialization entailed the differentiation of the rural work force into largely market-oriented entrepreneurs and landlords, increasingly market- and by-employment-oriented farmers, and a marginal class of small farmers, tenants, and landless workers able to remain in the village because of the nonagrarian economic opportunities increasingly available there. (Some, of course, migrated to the cities, but this flow decreased as protoindustrialization proceeded during the era.) Such differentiation implies a decline in community cohesion and an increase in the potential for social conflict, as do the monetization of the village economy and the commodification of land, labor, and other factors of production. At the same time, since collective political protest presupposed village unity, one might also expect that protoindustrialization would reduce the likelihood of protest.

The same implications arguably flow from the demographic results of protoindustrialization. As farmers produced increasingly for the market (and thus moved into nonfood production) and more and more individuals moved out of farming altogether, population pressure on the local food supply increased (especially in the towns and cities), in a context of both market-driven and climate-driven price volatility. Thus, although protoindustrialization enhanced macro-level economic conditions (partly because nonagricultural pursuits were undertaxed), it also entailed new forms of deprivation and insecurity, and thus did not necessarily reduce the potential for socioeconomic conflict. As one can see in early modern Europe, however, popular contention in response to food shortages and price fluctuations is relatively often focused on commercial, not governmental, agents; thus, again, the demography of protoindustrialization may well imply relatively less political protest.

Natural Adversity and Socioeconomic Constraint

Most salient in the picture seen by Japan's elites in the Tokugawa period were natural adversity and socioeconomic problems. Harsh climate and urban problems they could see easily, but population growth and economic prosperity seem to have escaped at least their control, if not their notice. The later Tokugawa period in particular witnessed an incessant litany of official dismay over swarms of migrant poor in the cities, depopulating villages, derelict farms, and the general deterioration of the land-tax-based fiscal structure of government. What accounts for the discrepancy? Are the conclusions based on the data above too rosy, or did social, economic, and political factors somehow transmute demographic recovery into social decay? Or was population change, a seeming harbinger of economic improvement, really a maleficent change in pressure or distribution?

The first of the phenomena viewed with alarm was natural disaster and its concomitant, famine. In a largely mountainous country, a preindustrial society in a northern temperate zone with capricious weather patterns, agriculture was always unpredictable; add to this an earthquake-prone, highly volcanic environment and alluvial plains susceptible to flooding, and it is unsurprising that crop failures were endemic. Topography made many such failures highly local, but poor transportation and a feudal polity meant that aid to distressed localities would not necessarily be forthcoming from neighboring domains (Umemura 1965:143–144). The results were sharp fluctuation of natural calamities across both time (see Figure 2) and space (see Figure 3), and famine as the era's "greatest social problem" (Umemura 1965:144).[2]

Figure 2 shows the sharp fluctuations in annual number of disasters; the decennial yearly averages illuminate the three major periods of calamity during the period under consideration: the Kyōhō famine in the 1730s, the Temmei famine in the 1780s, and the Tempō famine in the 1830s. As can be seen, these three decades did not necessarily witness the greatest number of calamities in any given year, but, insofar as such events had demographic or political implications, it is probable that

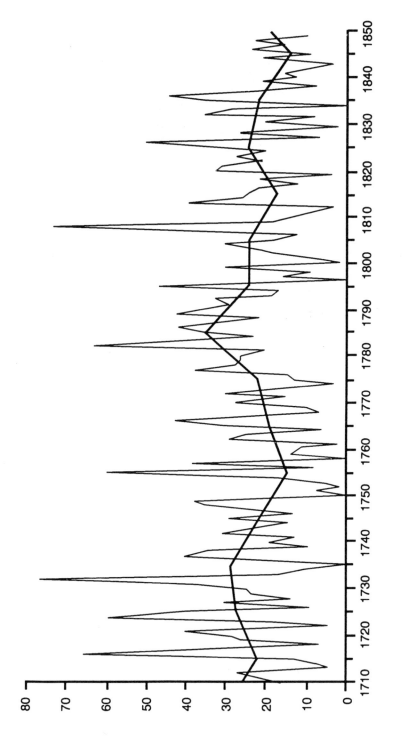

Figure 2. Number of provinces affected by natural disaster annually, and annual average per decade (source: Arakawa 1964:248–262).

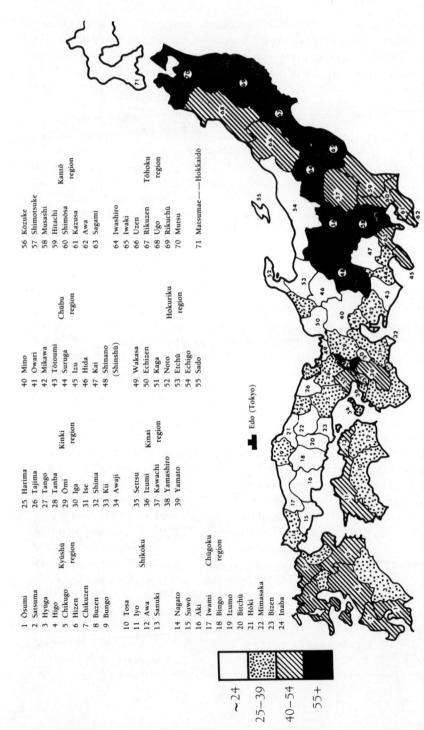

1 Ōsumi	25 Harima	40 Mino	56 Kozuke
2 Satsuma	26 Tajima	41 Owari	57 Shimotsuke
3 Hyūga	27 Tango	42 Mikawa	58 Musashi
4 Higo	28 Tanba	43 Tōtōumi	59 Hitachi
5 Chikugo	29 Ōmi	44 Suruga	60 Shimōsa	Kantō
6 Hizen	30 Iga	45 Izu	61 Kazusa	region
7 Chikuzen	Kyūshū	31 Ise	Kinki	46 Hida	62 Awa
8 Buzen	region	32 Shima	region	47 Kai	63 Sagami
9 Bungo	33 Kii	48 Shinano	
	34 Awaji	(Shinshū)	64 Iwashiro
10 Tosa			65 Iwaki
11 Iyo	35 Settsu	49 Wakasa	66 Uzen	Tōhoku
12 Awa	Shikoku	36 Izumi	Kinai	50 Echizen	67 Rikuzen	region
13 Sanuki	37 Kawachi	region	51 Kaga	68 Ugo
	38 Yamashiro	52 Noto	Hokuriku	69 Rikuchū
14 Nagato	39 Yamato	53 Etchū	region	70 Mutsu
15 Suwō		54 Echigo	
16 Aki		55 Sado	71 Matsumae——Hokkaidō
17 Iwami			
18 Bingo	Chūgoku		
19 Izumo	region		
20 Bitchū			
21 Hōki		Edo (Tokyo)	
22 Mimasaka			
23 Bizen			
24 Inaba			

~24
25–39
40–54
55+

Figure 3. Total natural disasters by province, 1590–1877 (source: Arakawa 1964:248–262)

protracted, perhaps cumulative, periods of dearth had greater significance than short, even if quite sharp, sequences of natural disasters. As also may be seen, however, the variation between decades was not extreme during the era: rural Japanese during these years lived constantly with the threat of crop failure and urbanites with the threat of constricted food supplies.

The distribution of these events was, however, quite uneven across the country. As seen in Figure 3, the most severely hit areas of Japan were the northeast, the central highlands of Shinano and Kōzuke, and Musashi province, home of Edo (which was particularly buffeted by fire and by famine, as a consequence of natural disaster elsewhere). The remainder of the Kantō region, parts of the Kinki region, and a belt stretching across northern Shikoku and covering most of Kyūshū were secondarily subject to harm. Western Honshū and, indeed, the entire western coast of Japan were relatively free of the chronic ravages of nature.

The demographic consequences of such disasters are not immediately clear, though the impact was greater the farther north one went (Kitō 1983b:80). The dips in the national population visible in Table 1 during the three periods of famine may be one, but concrete estimates of deaths from famine are marked by hyperbole, excitation, and not a little moral didacticism aimed at government policy or the inadequacy thereof. One estimate of deaths nationwide during the Temmei famine is 200,000 (Arakawa 1964:221ff.); in northern Nambu domain alone the toll may have exceeded 50,000 (Kitō 1983a:133). Considering starvation, infanticide, disease, reduced fertility, and delayed or prevented marriages, the depressive effect of each such famine on overall population was most likely of the order of several tens of thousands of persons at the least. Epidemics did not appear to play a major independent role in limiting population size (Jannetta 1987; Hayami 1982a: 72ff.), but in concert with the above they did contribute.

Another way in which natural disaster manifests itself demographically and politically is as a sudden increase in pressure on the food supply. The extent to which such increases (inferred from the frequency of disaster) are linked to magnitude of conflict will be seen below; for the moment we need only note that the best indicator of such increases in pressure—the price of rice, the staple food—was extremely sensitive to disasters. Figure 4 shows the average annual price of rice between 1721 and 1846 in the four cities of Hiroshima (Aki province), Ōsaka (Settsu province), Edo, and Aizu (Iwashiro province) and reveals both the sharp, short-term fluctuations typical of both prices and wages throughout the era (Umemura 1961) and the extraordinary increases of the 1730s,

1780s, and 1830s.[3] Disaggregating the data reveals still more (see Figure 5): when Hiroshima, in relatively disaster-free Aki province, is compared with Aizu in chronically ravaged Iwashiro, the range of fluctuation and the extreme highs are far greater in Aizu, and the overall level higher (with the exception of the Kyōhō famine, which struck western Japan with greater severity in the aftermath of a plague of locusts). The curves for Edo and Ōsaka are in between these two. Clearly, whatever effects they had on overall population, disasters had an immediate and region-ally specific effect on this indicator of the relationship between food sup-ply and demographic demand.

But quite apart from sporadic natural disaster, endemically harsh economic conditions have been adduced as explanatory factors in the stasis of Japan's national population during the Tokugawa era. Marxist historians assume exploitation and misery as givens in such a feudal sys-tem, and the process of protoindustrialization is also assumed to have spurred class differentiation and polarization as well as the creation of increasing numbers of tenant farmers and a rural "quasiproletariat" and an urban "protoproletariat," both immiserated (Mendels 1982; Tilly 1982; Ōuchi 1980; White 1989). And indeed the Japanese populace hardly lived comfortably: caloric intake seems to have approximated 1500 to 1700 daily (Nishikawa in Jansen and Rozman 1986; Mosk and Pak 1977; Kitō 1983a; Ōkawa 1976:18). More impressionistically, we have the account of Isabella Bird (1880:vol. 1, 167, and passim), a foreign visitor who roamed rural Japan during the early Meiji period and thought much of it "filthy and squalid beyond description." But her harshest commentary applied to northern, not central or southern Japan—she described the Kinki district (1880:vol. 2, 260–295) as "a lovely region of beauty, industry, and peace," a "highly luxurious coun-try" characterized by "thriving villages." And even in the north she noted (1880:vol.1) the discrepancy between the squalor and the industri-ousness: agricultural practices seemed advanced, the landscape itself was "one beautifully kept garden" with "splendid crops," and the people were "courteous, kindly, industrious" people who spent their evenings in enterprising "little economical ingenuities," that is, protoindustrial by-employments. Even the Tōhoku seems to have been to her more a place of extreme simplicity and dirt than one of poverty.

Thus bare survival at the edge of the starvation line does not seem to have characterized the mass of the rural peasantry, even in the north. Indeed, to the extent that protoindustrialization entailed proletarianiza-tion, it did so more in the cities than in the country (Saitō 1986:12). The misery-stagnation thesis loses almost all of the rest of its persuasive-ness in the face of incontrovertible data that show substantial macro-

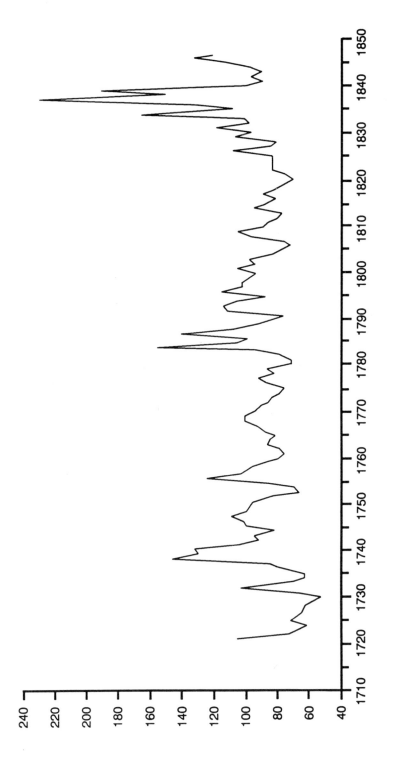

Figure 4.   Annual rice price: four-city average (1840–1848 = 100) (source: Iwahashi 1981)

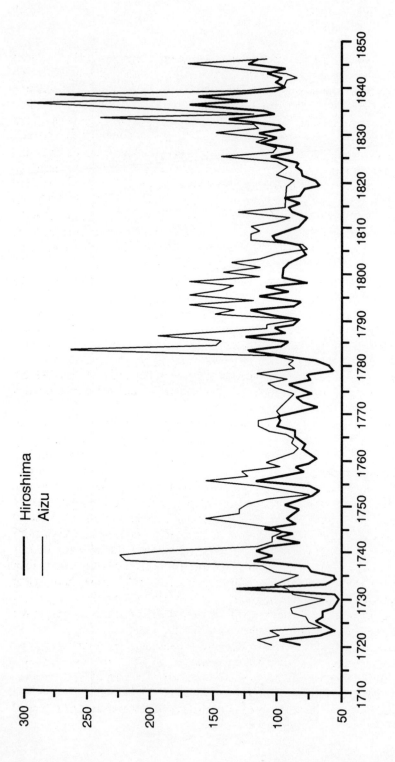

Figure 5. Annual rice price: Hiroshima and Aizu (1840–1848 = 100) (source: Iwahashi 1981)

level—and arguably even per-capita—economic growth during the latter half of the period either directly (Smith 1959; Hall and Jansen 1968:294; Hanley and Yamamura 1977; Saitō 1986; Umemura 1965; Hayami 1982b; Nishikawa 1979) or—through the surrogates of decreasing infant mortality, increasing life expectancy, decreasing age at marriage, and more equal sex ratios—indirectly (Hayami 1978:220; Kitō 1985; Masaoka et al. 1988; Umemura 1965:137). To the extent that population was voluntarily controlled, it appears to have been the result of conscious, calculated pursuit of higher standards of living, not misery and the fear of starvation (Smith 1977; Hanley and Yamamura 1977). In other words, millions of micro-level family size decisions based on family prosperity seem to have added up to a macro-level avoidance of overshooting the demographic carrying capacity of the Japanese environment (Kitō 1983b:86ff.). As economic growth continued in the nineteenth century, so also did demographic (again, with the stark exception of the Tempō period). Which was cause and which effect is unclear—the standard interpretation is that the economic growth makes the demographic possible, whereas scholars such as Saitō Osamu (1985; Mendels 1982:82) and Umemura Mataji (in Jansen and Rozman 1986:282–283) argue for a reverse relationship. For our purpose of observing the effects rather than the causes of growth, Hayami Akira's observation (in Jansen and Rozman 1986) that in fact the two proceeded hand-in-hand suffices.

Thus nature, at its extremes, appears to have affected population change on both the national and regional levels. The other major constraints on population were socioeconomic: first the apparent economic rationality at play in family establishment and size decisions just noted, and second the nature of Tokugawa-era urbanism. This last was not inconsiderable—not only was the shōgun's capital of Edo, with over 1 million people, the largest city in the world at the time, but almost 20 percent of the population lived in settlements of more than 3000 people (Jansen and Rozman 1986:323; the proportion in cities of 10,000 or more was c. 12–13 percent), making Japan one of the most urban societies in the early modern world. Nor was it trivial; as we have noted, Japan's cities were net consumers of population, and their process of change during the era influenced not only their own size, but that of the entire regions within which they were found.

The cities of the Tokugawa era experienced a period of rapid growth during the seventeenth century as the Tokugawa political economy—which featured the mandatory resettlement of the conspicuously consumerist samurai aristocracy in their lords' castle towns—took form. But in the eighteenth century the overall level of urbanism leveled

off, and many of the larger cities actually shrank as economic problems
and consequent government fiscal distress (and further consequent samurai impecuniousness) began to grow and the cities lost their economic
vitality (and demographic drawing power). The effects of earthquake,
fire, and disease were greater in denser settlements: Edo alone lost over
100,000 people in one fire and 130,000 in another, and some 250,000
in a cholera epidemic in 1858 (Kitō 1983b:155). Cities were also
characterized by large numbers of unmarried migrant workers, low marital rates, and short marital periods (Sekiyama 1959:85–86; Kitō
1983b:156; Toyoda 1962), all of which lowered fertility rates.

As the eighteenth century drew to a close and protoindustrialization
progressed, the national population recovered its growth trend, but the
cities did not. In fact, most continued either to dwindle or stagnate
(White 1981), while the rural (though not necessarily agricultural) population and that of the economically vital rural market towns grew.
Urbanization varied inversely with economic development, since the
wage differentials and job opportunities that lured migrants were more
attractive in the market towns than in the cities, which typically had as
their *raisons d'être* political rather than economic factors. One cause of
the discrepancy noted above between objective improvement and official
descriptions of decay may be that the elites were located in and based
their analyses on cities.

The contrasting demographic implications of politics and economics
may be seen most clearly if one examines the different types of cities and
towns of the Tokugawa era: metropolis, castle town, and market town.
The first type was epitomized by Edo and Ōsaka. Ōsaka was a purely
commercial city, home of the nation's largest rice exchange and center of
the national economy. With nothing to energize it but trade, it decayed
in direct relation to the feudal economy overall: from a high of almost
half a million inhabitants in the early eighteenth century, it fell to roughly
350,000 during the Temmei famine and declined almost monotonically
from then on, falling below 300,000 by 1840 and reaching 271,992 by
1873 (Yunoki and Horie 1930:200ff.). Edo had more forces sustaining it,
primarily the huge concentration of samurai (perhaps half a million of
them, including their families) surrounding the court of the shōgun plus
their huge support structure of service occupations (Saitō 1986). Consequently, it held its own, as Table 4 indicates, at a commoner population
of roughly half a million (and a total, including the uncounted samurai, of
one million plus: Sekiyama 1958, 1959; Tōkyō-fu 1935:96). After growing to this size from a small town in the late sixteenth century, it stag-
nated during the eighteenth century, after which it began to recover. All
of the figures in Table 4 are suggestive only—counting criteria changed

over time, many urbanites fell through the recorders' net, and the figures for 1843 and 1844 are clearly contradictory—but they suggest the Temmei famine, the recovery of the nineteenth century, and the sharp decline of the political twilight of the Tokugawa era, when thousands of the samurai, released from their fealty to the shōgun, departed the city. The data also purport to show the tremendous influx of refugees into Edo during the Tempō famine (Minami 1978:120; Kitajima 1966:419), but in fact no clear connection is apparent. The famine peaked in 1836; the city was already growing by the 1830s; even if the higher figures for 1843 and 1844 are the more accurate ones, they came several years after the famine; and the migrant proportion of Edo's population also peaked later, in 1843 (Minami 1978:133). Refugees would probably have been undocumented anyway, and one must look elsewhere for indications of their numbers.

The castle towns, domicile of the feudal lords and their samurai retinues (and, again, an occupational structure oriented thereto), tended to follow a course parallel to that of Edo: seventeenth-century growth, eighteenth-century decline, and in some cases nineteenth-century recovery. The population of Kōfu, capital of the province of Kai, is not atypical (see Table 5). Lucky enough to be located on a major highway between Edo and the Japan Sea coast, Kōfu shared in the economic activity of the nineteenth century, although the fastest-growing areas of the city at the end of the era were the densely packed rental housing neighborhoods associated in such cities with in-migrants and poverty (Tsuda 1978)—and with social unrest, as we shall see below. Indeed, of a recorded population of 13,951 in 1870, 6508 were categorized as poor (Tsuda 1978; *Kōfu Machikata* 1870).

Moving down the urban hierarchy to smaller towns, we find the same trend writ small, but with more exceptions, since these localities, like Ōsaka, had few political functions and were more purely influenced by economic trends. Towns on the edges of the metropolises, like Tennōji (an outlying part of Ōsaka), were unable to escape the currents pulling the metropolis down. From a peak population of 755 in 1806, Tennōji fell to a low of 438 in 1855. The inability of Tennōji to match the economic opportunities in more rural areas is shown by the drop in (usually migrant) servants in the town, from almost 100 at the turn of the century to only 5 in 1858 (Sasaki 1966; Hanley and Yamamura 1977:106ff.).

More distant towns were freer of the metropolitan vortex; those that fell victim to changing communication networks, silted harbors, or the regional division of labor and comparative advantage deriving from protoindustrialization faded (Fruin 1973), as others reversed the general

Table 4

The Population of Edo

Year	Population	Source	Year	Population	Source
1721	501,394	1	1840	551,369	3
1726	471,988	1	1841	563,689	4
1732	533,518	1	1842	551,063	4
1734	533,763	2	1843	577,677	4
1736	527,047	2		or	
1738	528,117	2		547,952	2
1743	501,166	2	1844	583,589	4
1747	512,913	2		or	
1786	457,083	4		559,497	3
1804	492,053	4	1845	557,698	4
1810	497,085	4	1849	564,943	3
1816	501,161	4	1850	559,115	3
1822	520,793	4	1854	570,898	4
1828	527,293	4	1855	564,544	4
1832	545,623	4	1861	562,505	4
1834	522,754	4	1867	539,618	4

SOURCES: (1) Sekiyama 1959:114; (2) Sekiyama 1958:221, 227; (3) Minami 1978:55, 90, 133; (4) Tōkyō-fu 1935:93ff., 115–118.

Table 5

The Population of Kōfu

Year	Population	Source	Year	Population	Source
1670	12,772	1	1762	13,029	2
1689	14,334	1	1764	12,248	2
1697	13,539	1	1786	11,677	2
1705	13,291	2	1798	11,052	2
1710	13,306	1	1806	9,566	1
1720	13,662	2	1836	9,946	3
1724	14,006	2	1844	10,448	3
1744	12,975	2	1858	11,992	4
1750	13,730	2	1864	11,071	2
1756	12,872	2			

SOURCES: (1) *Kōfu Ryakushi* 19:214–217; (2) Iida 1976: 416; (3) Iida 1979: 16; (4) Kōfu Machi Bugyō, *Goyō Nikki* (personal communication from Iida Bunya, July 1979).

urban malaise and began to grow in the nineteenth century. Hirano and Hanakuma, in the hinterlands of Ōsaka and Hyōgo, respectively, show such a pattern; Hirano in particular, after peaking at over 10,000 people in the early eighteenth century, dropped (because of the course change of a river and the loss of the cotton monopoly by its own region) to 7500 by the 1820s, whereupon it reversed and (with a short but sharp drop during the Tempō period) demonstrated gradual growth, exceeding 8000 inhabitants by the end of the Tokugawa era (Tsuda 1970:258ff.; Hanley and Yamamura 1977:106ff.).

Even more distant, economically relatively autonomous, towns showed even greater vitality: in a study of 43 villages and towns in one region, Hayami Akira (1978) found trends of demographic increase at the end of the Tokugawa era in 35, and many had at that time their maximum populations. Isolated studies of regions like Suwa (Hayami 1973b) and towns like Hida province's Takayama (Sasaki 1969, 1978) corroborate the picture, lending empirical substance to the impressionistic records of the time that contrast the bustle and prosperity of the rural towns with the empty houses, decreasing numbers of in-migrant servants and hired help, and widespread poverty of the major cities.

Such characterizations lead us toward a final aspect of Tokugawa urbanism—its structure—and suggest in turn two final considerations in our overview of the demographic history of the era: migration and population as political factors. Structurally, Tokugawa-era towns and cities were characterized by what I shall refer to below (from a clearly political perspective) as large vulnerable populations—that is, concentrations of largely proletarianized people who did not produce their own food and were therefore dependent on farmers, shippers, and a variety of merchants for their sustenance. As we shall see in greater detail shortly, they included large migrant populations—indeed, as noted, towns survived only insofar as they could attract such migrants—concentrated in lower-status occupations and typically in low-quality rental housing. Sasaki Junnosuke estimates (1974:66ff.) that roughly one-half of the urban population was lower-class, with the proportion higher in the three biggest cities of Edo, Ōsaka, and Kyōto; in a study of several neighborhoods in Edo, Minami Kazuo (1978) found that between one-third and one-half were home renters, day laborers and other unskilled workers, categorized poor, or combinations of these; probably less than a quarter were propertied townspeople (*chōnin*) (Saitō Osamu, personal communication). In the town of Takayama cited above, renters numbered 70 to 80 percent of all resident families and some 90 percent of these were *mutaka*, or without income-producing property (Kojima 1979:53ff.).

Finally, the cities and towns contained variable numbers of the samurai aristocracy. In Edo they probably equaled the commoner population, amounting to some half million. In the castle towns, where the rest of them were required to live, they constituted anywhere from a quarter to well over half of the population (Fujioka 1966:197ff.; Sekiyama 1948:235). In other localities they were almost nonexistent. This concentration of the ruling class in the cities, one might expect, would contribute to a tightness of administrative grip found elsewhere (Skinner 1979) to dampen the level of popular collective action; whether it had this effect in Japan we shall see.

People on the Move

The concentration in the cities of the "working and dangerous" classes (Chevalier 1958) might well have had the opposite effect. That these classes were largely migrant—owing to the demographic dynamics of the cities noted above—accentuates our interest in the migration to which the cities owed their sustenance. The dependence of cities on a constant stream of in-migrants eases our task—at least on the impressionistic level—of measuring migrant flows, since such flows can be inferred quite directly from the demographic fortunes of the cities. The same kind of measurement is not possible in the countryside, since natural increase and decrease played a larger role in demographic change, but a number of case studies of the phenomenon provide us with some information.

Overall, Tokugawa Japan appears to have been characterized by large migrant flows, although with the spread of economic opportunity to more and more rural areas through the agency of protoindustrialization, gross migration seems to have diminished, at least in the nineteenth century. This trend is most clearly visible in the biggest city, Edo, both in terms of migration there from specific rural areas (Hayami 1973b; Fruin 1973) and in terms of the migrant population of Edo itself: in the second quarter of the century roughly 30 percent of the population were migrants, but by the end of the era the proportion had shrunk to roughly one-fifth (Sekiyama 1958; 1959; H. Smith 1981:8). Simultaneously the number of temporary migrant workers (*dekasegi*) dropped from almost 35,000 to less than 5000 (H. Smith 1981:8), and the sex ratio approached 1:1—since the majority of migrants were male, this is a further indicator of decreased migrant inflow.

The data on six neighborhoods compiled by Minami Kazuo (1978) fill out this picture in several respects. The migrant proportions of these neighborhoods ranged from 20 to 30 percent, with one exception at 44 percent; as noted, lower-class occupations and living conditions were especially common among the migrants. And overall mobility rates were quite high, both among migrants and native Edoites. But the migrants did not fulfill an image of rootless youth: they were by and large older, and more often married than the native populations of these lower-class areas. Such socially established migrants accounted for between 40 percent and 100 percent of the migrants in the six neighborhoods. This high proportion might simply reflect the dropoff in in-migration in the 1850s and 1860s (were the single and the young freer to move back to the country?). At any rate, we should not expect a migrant rabble to figure prominently in whatever collective contention might occur in the metropolis.

When we shift our gaze from Edo to the provincial towns, again we see high but diminishing rates of gross migration (or at least temporary work-related movement) that were closely linked to population change: in many such places social, rather than natural, increase and decrease drove demographic change (Tsuda 1977:101, 1970:264ff.; Sasaki 1966, 1969; Hanley and Yamamura 1977:177ff.). Simply put, net out-migration varied inversely with population size: whenever economic conditions perked up, so did in-migration, and growing populations were thus almost invariably accompanied by net in-migration. They were also accompanied by decreasing gross migration, since most of the available labor pool was found in the villages, and it tended to move less and less as local by-employment opportunities multiplied in a growing economy.

Urban and village patterns also differed: in the case of towns it was decreased in-migration that contributed most to net outflow; in villages net outflow was mainly the result of increased out-migration (Tsuda 1970, 1977; Hayami 1973a, 1975; Hanley 1973; Fruin 1973). But in both cases the relationship between economic conditions and movement was the reverse of what one sees in modern societies: prosperity seems to have depressed migration in Tokugawa Japan, at least after rural-centered protoindustrialization set in. And what migration did continue was decreasingly directed toward the bigger cities: Edo and castle towns in general became less attractive destinations than the economically livelier smaller towns (Hayami 1973a, 1973b; Fruin 1973; Kitō 1983b:163; Hanley 1973).

Thus Tokugawa Japan appears to have been characterized by distinctive patterns of migration, the selectivity, direction of flow, and volume of which may have implications for the sorts of social behavior we shall examine below. The primary motive for movement was economic, even more so than is the case in modern societies where education (for oneself and one's children), noneconomic urban amenities, and transfers by employers (including the military) also loom large. One need not subscribe to a Marxist viewpoint to agree that living standards were low in much of the countryside and that out-migration was one response thereto along with birth control and delayed marriage (Hayami 1975:232). Individual rural out-migrants were disproportionately from poorer or landless families, and ecologically out-migration was also associated with high tax rates (Fruin 1973; Kishimoto 1961).

In other words, in this society, like other premodern ones, the "push" of rural poverty outweighed the "pull" of urban jobs, amenities, and bright lights. Consequently, the selectivity of rural out-migration was negative, i.e., the poorer elements in the village were "pushed" hardest toward departure by both continual hardship and sporadic natural disasters (White 1979:166). That migration was push-driven also meant that changes in rural conditions were a more powerful explanatory factor in migration than changes in urban. Most significantly, eighteenth- and nineteenth-century protoindustrial by-employments acted increasingly as a "brake" on out-migration from the villages (Saitō, chapter in Jansen and Rozman 1986). The demographic health of towns and cities was at the mercy of such forces. Still, the pull of urban economic opportunities cannot be dismissed, especially toward the end of the era when cuts in samurai stipends, bakufu and domain fiscal crises, and high urban inflation combined to cut the urban demand for labor (Hayami 1988:201).

Thus the relationships between settlement size, migration, and economic conditions were as follows: economic growth in the villages depressed out-migration and enhanced natural growth (through both increased fertility and decreased mortality); depressed out-migration also contributed to population increase. In towns, on the one hand, economic growth meant natural increase and net in-migration, and the net in-migration in turn contributed to overall growth in the population. In cities, on the other hand, the prevailing rural locus of economic growth meant decreased in-migration; it also led to increased natural growth, but not enough to maintain city size. So, unless a city had some way of getting on the protoindustrial bandwagon—as an entrepôt or center of finance or uniquely advantaged manufacturing center—or had some political functions to attract population, macro-level economic growth meant at best urban economic and demographic stagnation. Consequently, we should not be surprised to find macro-level economic growth alongside significant urban social unrest. This is not to say that the countryside will be quiescent—the relatively deprived who now can stay in the village will not necessarily, by virtue of their protoindustrial occupation, get out of their disadvantaged position. But it is quite possible that should such people contest their status, they will direct their actions not toward political institutions, but toward the economic structures that control their lives. Thus the complex interplay of economy and demography may have not only quantitative but qualitative effects as well on popular contention.

The Politics of Population

We have thus far alluded to the hypothetical implications of population change for both social and political conflict derived from the research of numerous scholars and a few of the implications suggested by an overview of Tokugawa demographic history. A national overview might lead to premature dismissal of population change as a major causal factor in contention, since neither size, density, nor distribution changed dramatically during most of the Tokugawa period (at least the period after 1700). Regional and intraurban change were considerable, however, and Japan's feudal character lent special meaning to changes from one area to another. And the whole was overlaid after the late eighteenth century with a process of regionally uneven economic growth. Thus we should recall that regional population *size* increased in most regions at most times; curiously, most Japanese historians associate popular contention with demographic decrease, with poverty the ultimate cause of both in the northeast, and urbanism and its attendant "protoproletarianization" the causes in the Kantō and Kinki. *Density* thus increased marginally (except in times of dearth and places of great urban settlement, and even many of these latter began to grow toward the end of the era); in the popular mind, however, both high density (in the big cities) and low (in the northeast) are linked to contention. *Pressure* on the food supply overall decreased as economic growth outstripped demographic, although the vulnerable nonagricultural population grew substantially in both town and country; thus food supply and demand became spatially incongruent, with conflict a hypothetical result—and yet, again, one might assume that the depopulated Tōhoku would enjoy the most diminished pressure on its own (at worst stable, but probably also growing) food supply. And *distribution*, although stable at a very high level of urbanism for such a society (Jansen and Rozman 1986:ch. 12), can be broken down into metropolitan stagnation and small-town vitality, although both were characterized by large seams of poverty that were both feared and targeted by elites. Demographic *crises* were frequent and likely to have contentious consequences, since they were closely tied to food prices and could be markedly alleviated by official relief or markedly exacerbated by official refusal to lighten or delay exactions temporarily. The feudal political structure enhanced the distribution problem and added a demonstration effect: in Sōma domain almost 15 percent of the total population either starved to death or fled during the famine year of 1783; in neighboring Shirakawa not a single death from famine was recorded (Kitō 1983b:133).

The political significance of population change lay not only in its potential influence on social behavior, but in its role in the eyes of the ruling class and its consequent role in public policy. The various feudal governments (located in the cities) associated demographic change with problems, either the fiscal decay that attended what they saw as rural depopulation (but was in fact mostly "deagrarianization") or urban social unrest, which led to frequent efforts to expel migrants from the cities and highly draining relief efforts.[4]

Rural "depopulation" was attacked directly, though pronatalist policies and invitations from low-population domains to new settlers (Sekiyama 1948), and indirectly, since it was vainly hoped that migrants expelled from the cites would return to the land. The first antivagabond decree was issued in 1709, but it was only in the latter half of the century that concerted efforts began to limit movement to Edo and other large cities (Minami 1978:123ff.). Some were voluntary; the most famous set, issued by Mizuno Tadakuni in 1842–1843, banned further inmigration to Edo and expelled those without families and permanent jobs from there and elsewhere and did have a temporarily depressive effect on at least the migrant populations of Edo and Ōsaka (Minami 1978:160ff.; Sekiyama 1959:228–229; Kitajima 1966:445–446; Beasley 1967:27). Other observers, however (Honjo 1935:176; Tōkyō Hyakunen 1973:vol. 1, 1341), question the efficacy of the edicts, and at any rate they became dead letters when Mizuno was fired in late 1843.

Relief was both more efficacious—the literature abounds with stories of rich merchants who saved their homes, shops, and wealth with either preemptive distributions of money, food, and drink to the local poor or effusive payoffs to riotous crowds—and more frequent. It was also a serious fiscal burden: the government of Edo alone distributed relief to people by the hundreds of thousands almost every year during the 1830s, exceeding 50,000 *koku* of rice on several occasions (Tōkyō Hyakunen 1973:vol. 1, 1255ff., 1590–1591; Hyakushō Ikki 1980:334–335; 50,000 koku was approximately the entire annual productive capacity of the domain of a medium-sized feudal lord). The figures make it appear that at least half of the commoner population of Edo was on relief at numerous times during the decade.[5] The motives for this largess were hardly humanitarian, although the government did ideally ascribe to Confucian prescriptions of benevolent rule. The government had a perception, common to regimes in other ages and settings, of the urban unwashed—mobile and unaccounted-for, penurious, and explosive—as a political factor of the greatest significance, and it acted on this perception at every turn.

Contention: Forms and Frequencies of Collective Action
The Quality of Contention

Contrary to common images of Japan as a distinctively harmonious and nonconflictual society, the Tokugawa era witnessed a considerable volume of popular contention of various types, most of it undocumented. The most complete record of the era, Aoki Kōji's *Hyakushō Ikki Sōgō Nempyō* (1981), includes over 7500 incidents: over 500 cases of petition and litigation between commoners and by commoners against the government; over 3500 conflicts within the commoner class (many of which were food riots and other protests by lower-status commoners against higher); another 1000 or more cases of such social conflict that eventuated in overtures to the government for intervention of some kind; and over 2000 protests by commoners against institutions, agents, or policies of the central shōgunate government or the government of one or more of the feudal domains.

Aoki's data on political protest and public litigation are regarded as essentially complete, but those on social conflict and the politically transformed social conflicts have to be underrepresentative—it is difficult to believe that any of Japan's 60,000 to 80,000 villages went for the entire 268 years of the era without any such conflict.[6] Although Aoki's data on social conflict are a sample, not the universe, of such conflict, the spatial and temporal distribution of the data and the trends therein over time relative to the better-documented political conflict can be examined usefully (for a fuller discussion of the Aoki data see Appendix and White 1989).

In general, both social and political conflict—even the largest rebellions—were defensive and restorative, not revolutionary: their goal was the reestablishment of a universally accepted (by both rulers and subjects) moral-economic order. They were instrumental and concrete in their goals: apocalyptic visions and systemic change were not sought; tangible and immediate relief, remedy, and improvements in life and living standard were. They were explicit in their demands. They were almost always nonviolent toward people, even in the *uchikowashi* (lit., smashings), or riots, where the homes, shops, warehouses, property, and even personal possessions of merchants, moneylenders, and the rapacious or insensitive wealthy were shredded, reduced to kindling, strewn about, burned, or forcibly appropriated or sold at a popularly determined "just price." They were also most often well organized (and frequently

planned well in advance), not moblike: examples abound of incidents
planned for weeks or months ahead of time, touched off by prearranged
signals, and involving large numbers of individuals organized by village of
residence and bound by mutually-agreed-upon principles of correct
behavior (for overviews of these qualities see Aoki M. et al. 1981; Vlastos
1986; Walthall 1986; Fukaya 1979; Yokoyama 1977).

Within these commonalities, a variety of forms of collective behavior
characterized the commoners' repertoire. Some of these have been
artificially enshrined in the common terminology of the literature, but
they serve to draw general distinctions. The most general category of
conflict was the *hyakushō ikki,* or *ikki,* usually conceived of as a confrontation between commoners and the government (and thus putatively a
form of class struggle). There were several types (in roughly increasing
order of disruptiveness): *chōsan* (collective flight of peasants to escape
misrule), *fuon* (minor unrest implying discontent with current policies or
conditions), *shūso* (presentation of demands or petitions to officials), *osso*
or *jikiso* (an "end run" or appeal directly to a higher level of government
than that closest to the people, usually after being rebuffed on first over-
ture), *gōso* (collective demonstration and belligerent confrontation with
authorities), *uchikowashi,* and *hōki* (full-blown rebellion, often involving
more than one feudal domain and running into the tens of thousands of
participants although, again, rarely involving weapons of any kind). The
less extreme forms of *ikki* were legal, either explicitly or ambiguously;
osso, gōso, and *hōki,* however, were dealt with harshly as contraventions
of the feudal order, whatever their substantive merits (for discussion of
these distinctions see Yokoyama 1977; Bix 1986).

In addition to *ikki* —a fuzzy category which as we have already seen
included the *uchikowashi,* which were in fact social conflicts and not
political protest—the major forms of contention, conventionally
classified, included the *murakata sōdō,* or village dispute, which occurred
either within villages (e.g., between tax-collecting headmen and villagers)
or between them (e.g., over water or common-land rights); the *kokuso,* or
(legal) provincial appeal, which usually involved groups of merchants liti-
gating against the privileges of other merchants or against government
regulation of their activities; and the *yonaoshi,* or world-renewal rebellion (Scheiner 1973; Sasaki J. 1973, 1979; Najita and Koschmann
1982:164ff.), an intense and sometimes millenarian form of intraclass conflict directed at better-off peasants-cum-merchants-cum-village
officials, which was stimulated by the chaotic economic and political conditions of the last years of the Tokugawa period and was aimed at a
downward redistribution of wealth and power. The *yonaoshi* were closer
to system-changing (as opposed to system-reinforcing or restoring)

conflict than anything preceding them during the era, but whether they were intrinsically forward- or backward-looking is a matter of debate.

There are two problems with the typology sketched out above. In the first place, the relative magnitude of the different types of events is not self-evident. Second, the categories themselves often reflect only narrowly the quality of the events involved. Some derive only from the legal terminology of the time—for example, to the Tokugawa authorities the most important aspects of contention were whether it reflected deliberate concertation (*totō*) and whether it contravened regular channels of remonstrance (e.g., *osso* or *jikiso*). But these distinctions were made without any regard for cause, magnitude, participants, or quality of contention, in the same way that a "riot" in early modern England was simply a legal category, a contentious event whose participants, after having had the Riot Act read to them, still refused to disperse. At the other extreme are the *kokuso* and *yonaoshi*, which imply specific actors, targets, and objectives. In yet other cases the derivation of the categories is even less helpful: two of Aoki's major types are urban and rural contention (*toshi sōjō* and *murakata sōdō*), the criteria for which are simply locational.

Efforts have been made to remedy the first problem by weighting types of events in ascending order of magnitude (Yokoyama 1977; Sugimoto 1975, 1978). A similar operation has been applied here to the Aoki data, the basic data source for this study, by calculating the magnitude of each type of event as a combination of its scope (in number of villages and participants involved and its duration) and aggressiveness (in terms of participants' behavior and the destruction of property or injury of persons; see Appendix).

The creation of new categories has been attempted less often; in this study I have used legality, aggressiveness, and intra- or interclass nexus of contention as criteria in creating empirical, rather than simply legal or spatial, categories of collective action (see Appendix). The result is four classes of contention: petition and litigation, social conflict, political conflict (those social conflicts eventuating in political actions), and political protest. These four types of action, with each event weighted for its magnitude, will be our objects of examination, along with the total magnitude of conflict occurring in different spaces and times.

The theoretical rationale for this typology is threefold. First, both legality/illegality and interclass verticality reflect the assumption that whether or not conflict impinges upon the (coercive) state has powerful implications for its consequences and, hence, for the individual and collective calculi that precede it. Second, intra- or interclass nexus reflects the assumption that the extent to which groups of commoners contend among themselves as equals, contend with their betters, or directly challenge the state reflects class structure, the salience of the state in society, the cohesion of communities, and the course of economic change. Third, aggressiveness hypothetically reflects the quality of both intraclass and state-society relationships and, again, has far-reaching implications for impact and state response (DeNardo 1985). The data indicate *who* acted vis-à-vis *whom,* and *how;* my assumption was that categories based on these three pieces of knowledge would differ across multiple dimensions of explanation and meaning.

These categories do not imply different objectives or goals held by either the challengers or their targets in particular forms of contention. For one thing, many actions had multiple objectives—commoner manifestoes of twenty or thirty separate grievances were not rare. Therefore, for example, the "political" in political protest refers to actors, not objectives. That is, the approach of this study is structural, and the initial assumption is that different groups living within certain structures— economic, social, and state—under different circumstances will adopt different contentious means to pursue similar goals. Thus, under some circumstances commoners might attack a merchant or village headman over the conversion rate (for tax purposes) of rice into coin, whereas in other circumstances a protest to domain or bakufu officials might be lodged. In many instances the class composition of the actors, the circumstances under which they act, and their stated demands permit inference of their motivations, but the relationship of objectives or goals to categories of contention is an empirical question, not part of the categories themselves.

Causes and Goals

The motivations of contenders cross-cut the social and political forms of conflict presented above. In general, conflict had three sources: economic, fiscal, and administrative. Economic causes involved dearth and high consumer or low producer prices; the rapacity of merchants, moneylenders, and landlords; high interest rates; and hoarding of food. Fiscal reasons included excessive taxation or tax assessments; changes in form, medium, or timing of extraction; changes in money supply or exchange rates; government regulation of economic activity; conflicts over guild and monopoly privileges, corvée burdens, and a host of other complaints. Administrative causes included misfeasance, malfeasance, and nonfeasance by both commoner officials in the village and domainial or shōgunal officials at higher levels of the system—bribery, misappropriation of tax money or community property, dishonest application of tax quotas, merchant-official collusion, insensitivity and arbitrariness,

excessive numbers of officials (supported by the people's taxes), oligarch-
ical elitism in selection of village officials, unequal or inequitable application of law, and so forth. Again, the targets of popular contention could
be in either the commoner or samurai class, and respite could be sought
from either. Acquisition of food, seed, and money; price and tax reduc-
tions or equalization; trade liberalization within village or domain; and
discipline or removal of unjust noble or commoner officials were only a
few of the goals.

Tokugawa Japan was an autocratic polity in an agrarian society, but
neither exploitation nor poverty alone explains the volume of contention
that characterized the era. Government oppression and sparse existence
were constants and cannot explain variations in popular behavior
(Kokushō 1971; Hayashi 1976). Most often a stepping away from established practices in welfare and relief, taxation levels and forms, and
administration—especially the failure of the governing or mercantile
strata to curb corruption, allow free economic activity, or take short-term
dearth into account—was the provocation for protest against both commoner and samurai elites. Thus our attention will be directed toward
both times and places in which there was variation in established political and economic factors.

The Distribution of Conflict

Figures 6 through 10 depict the magnitudes of the different types of contention in each province for the entire Tokugawa period and the total
magnitude of all types. These data are adjusted for provincial size—they
are not precisely per-capita, which is the ideal, but are calculated on a
per-koku basis.[7] Three features of the figures are especially noteworthy.

First, it is clear that the different forms of conflict are related—the
provinces that rank high in one tend to rank high in the others, and vice
versa.[8] Petition and litigation are moderately strongly related to all of the
other forms; social conflict and political conflict are the most strongly
related (unsurprisingly, since the latter is an outgrowth of the former);
and political protest is relatively distinct from all of the other forms of
contention. It is interesting that the clearest differences are not between
the legal activities of petition and litigation and the others. In particular,
litigation in the form of the *kokuso* has been most frequently discussed in
the context of the advanced mercantile organizations of the Kinai, but as
one can see here, it was just as frequent in other widely separated parts
of the country, including the Tōhoku and mountainous core of the Chūbu
and a scattering of provinces along the western coast of the Sea of Japan.
Provinces that rank high in contention across the board include Rikuchū
in the far northeast, a large block of provinces centering on mountainous

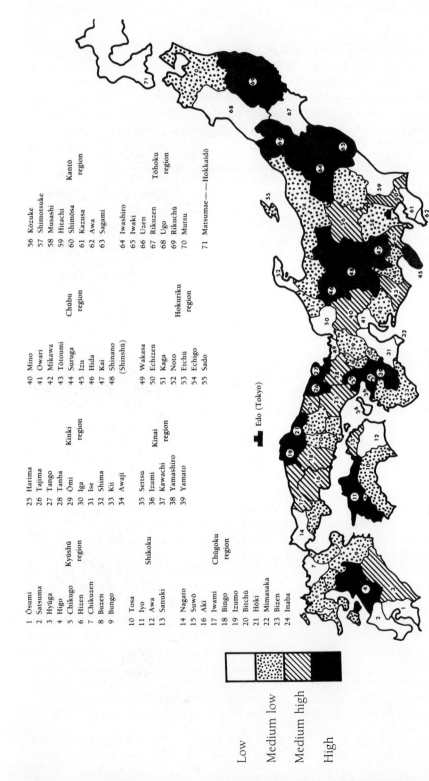

Figure 6. Magnitude of petition and litigation, 1590–1877

1 Ōsumi
2 Satsuma
3 Hyūga
4 Higo
5 Chikugo
6 Hizen
7 Chikuzen
8 Buzen
9 Bungo

Kyūshū region

10 Tosa
11 Iyo
12 Awa
13 Sanuki

Shikoku

14 Nagato
15 Suwō
16 Aki
17 Iwami
18 Bingo
19 Izumo
20 Bitchū
21 Hōki
22 Mimasaka
23 Bizen
24 Inaba

Chūgoku region

25 Harima
26 Tajima
27 Tango
28 Tanba
29 Ōmi
30 Iga
31 Ise
32 Shima
33 Kii
34 Awaji

Kinki region

35 Settsu
36 Izumi
37 Kawachi
38 Yamashiro
39 Yamato

Kinai region

40 Mino
41 Owari
42 Mikawa
43 Tōtoumi
44 Suruga
45 Izu
46 Hida
47 Kai
48 Shinano (Shinshū)

Chūbu region

49 Wakasa
50 Echizen
51 Kaga
52 Noto
53 Etchū
54 Echigo
55 Sado

Hokuriku region

56 Kōzuke
57 Shimotsuke
58 Musashi
59 Hitachi
60 Shimōsa
61 Kazusa
62 Awa
63 Sagami

Kantō region

64 Iwashiro
65 Iwaki
66 Uzen
67 Rikuzen
68 Ugo
69 Rikuchū
70 Mutsu

Tōhoku region

71 Matsumae——Hokkaidō

Edo (Tokyo)

Low

Medium low

Medium high

High

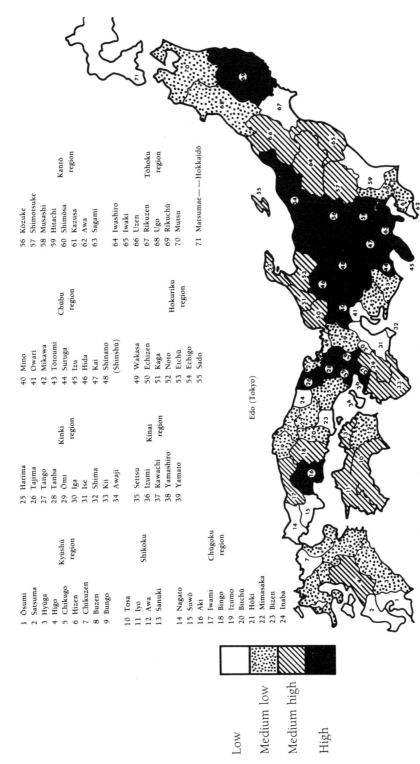

					Kinki	Chūbu		Kantō
1 Ōsumi	25 Harima			40 Mino	region	region		region
2 Satsuma	26 Tajima			41 Owari				
3 Hyūga	27 Tango			42 Mikawa			56 Kōzuke	
4 Higo	28 Tanba			43 Tōtōumi			57 Shimotsuke	
5 Chikugo	Kyūshū	29 Ōmi	Kinki	44 Suruga			58 Musashi	
6 Hizen	region	30 Iga	region	45 Izu			59 Hitachi	
7 Chikuzen		31 Ise		46 Hida			60 Shimōsa	
8 Buzen		32 Shima		47 Kai			61 Kazusa	
9 Bungo		33 Kii		48 Shinano			62 Awa	
		34 Awaji		(Shinshū)			63 Sagami	
10 Tosa		35 Settsu		49 Wakasa			64 Iwashiro	Tōhoku
11 Iyo	Shikoku	36 Izumi	Kinai	50 Echizen			65 Iwaki	region
12 Awa		37 Kawachi	region	51 Kaga			66 Uzen	
13 Sanuki		38 Yamashiro		52 Noto			67 Rikuzen	
		39 Yamato		53 Etchū	Hokuriku		68 Ugo	
14 Nagato				54 Echigo	region		69 Rikuchū	
15 Suwō				55 Sado			70 Mutsu	
16 Aki								
17 Iwami	Chūgoku						71 Matsumae——Hokkaidō	
18 Bingo	region							
19 Izumo								
20 Bitchū								
21 Hōki								
22 Mimasaka				Edo (Tokyo)				
23 Bizen								
24 Inaba								

Low

Medium low

Medium high

High

Figure 7. Magnitude of social conflict, 1590–1877

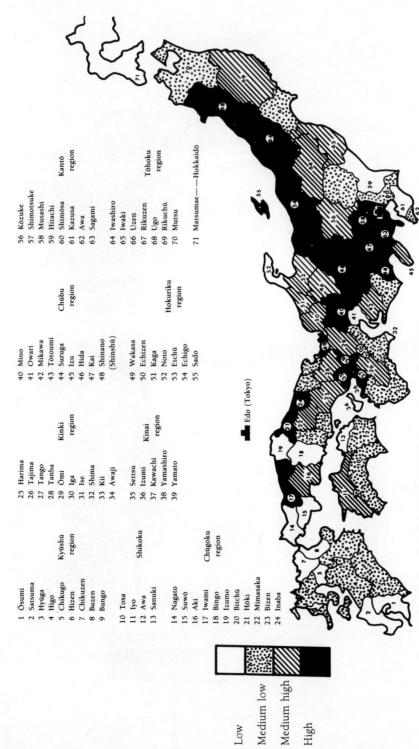

1 Ōsumi	25 Harima	40 Mino	56 Kōzuke
2 Satsuma	26 Tajima	41 Owari	57 Shimotsuke
3 Hyūga	27 Tango	42 Mikawa	58 Musashi
4 Higo	28 Tanba	43 Tōtoumi	59 Hitachi
5 Chikugo	29 Ōmi	44 Suruga	60 Shimōsa
6 Hizen	30 Iga	45 Izu	61 Kazusa
7 Chikuzen	31 Ise	46 Hida	62 Awa
8 Buzen	32 Shima	47 Kai	63 Sagami
9 Bungo	33 Kii	48 Shinano	64 Iwashiro
	34 Awaji	(Shinshū)	65 Iwaki
10 Tosa			66 Uzen
11 Iyo	35 Settsu	49 Wakasa	67 Rikuzen
12 Awa	36 Izumi	50 Echizen	68 Ugo
13 Sanuki	37 Kawachi	51 Kaga	69 Rikuchū
	38 Yamashiro	52 Noto	70 Mutsu
14 Nagato	39 Yamato	53 Etchū	
15 Suwō		54 Echigo	71 Matsumae——Hokkaidō
16 Aki		55 Sado	
17 Iwami			
18 Bingo			
19 Izumo			
20 Bitchū			
21 Hōki			
22 Mimasaka			
23 Bizen			
24 Inaba			

Kyūshū region

Shikoku

Chūgoku region

Kinki region

Kinai region

Chūbu region

Hokuriku region

Kantō region

Tōhoku region

Edo (Tokyo)

Low

Medium low

Medium high

High

Figure 8. Magnitude of political conflict, 1590–1877

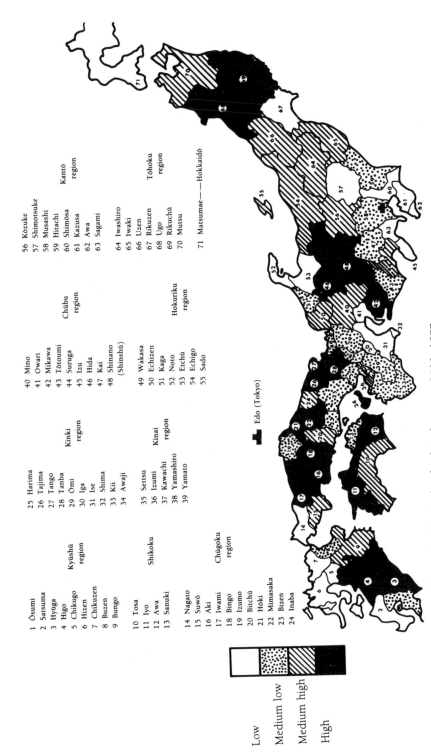

1 Ōsumi	25 Harima	40 Mino	56 Kōzuke
2 Satsuma	26 Tajima	41 Owari	57 Shimotsuke
3 Hyūga	27 Tango	42 Mikawa	58 Musashi
4 Higo	28 Tamba	43 Tōtoumi	59 Hitachi
5 Chikugo	29 Ōmi	44 Suruga	60 Shimōsa
6 Hizen	Kinki	30 Iga	Chūbu	45 Izu	61 Kazusa	Kantō
7 Chikuzen	region	31 Ise	region	46 Hida	62 Awa	region
8 Buzen	32 Shima	47 Kai	63 Sagami
9 Bungo	33 Kii	48 Shinano
34 Awaji	(Shinshū)	64 Iwashiro
10 Tosa	65 Iwaki
11 Iyo	35 Settsu	49 Wakasa	66 Uzen
12 Awa	Shikoku	36 Izumi	Kinai	50 Echizen	67 Rikuzen	Tōhoku
13 Sanuki	37 Kawachi	region	51 Kaga	68 Ugo	region
38 Yamashiro	Hokuriku	52 Noto	69 Rikuchū
14 Nagato	39 Yamato	region	53 Etchū	70 Mutsu
15 Suwō	54 Echigo
16 Aki	Chugoku	55 Sado	71 Matsumae——Hokkaidō
17 Iwami	region
18 Bingo
19 Izumo
20 Bitchū
21 Hōki	Edo (Tokyo)
22 Mimasaka
23 Bizen
24 Inaba

Low
Medium low
Medium high
High

Figure 9. Magnitude of political protest, 1590–1877

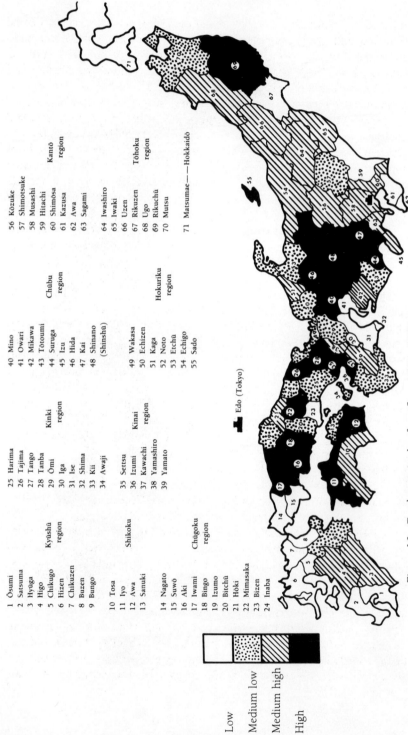

1 Ōsumi	25 Harima	40 Mino	56 Kōzuke	
2 Satsuma	26 Tajima	41 Owari	57 Shimotsuke	
3 Hyūga	27 Tango	42 Mikawa	58 Musashi	
4 Higo	28 Tanba	43 Tōtoumi	59 Hitachi	
5 Chikugo	29 Ōmi	44 Suruga	60 Shimōsa	Kantō
6 Hizen Kyūshū	30 Iga Kinki	45 Izu Chūbu	61 Kazusa	region
7 Chikuzen region	31 Ise region	46 Hida region	62 Awa	
8 Buzen	32 Shima	47 Kai	63 Sagami	
9 Bungo	33 Kii	48 Shinano		
	34 Awaji	(Shinshū)	64 Iwashiro	
10 Tosa			65 Iwaki	
11 Iyo	35 Settsu	49 Wakasa	66 Uzen	Tōhoku
12 Awa Shikoku	36 Izumi Kinai	50 Echizen	67 Rikuzen	region
13 Sanuki	37 Kawachi region	51 Kaga Hokuriku	68 Ugo	
	38 Yamashiro	52 Noto region	69 Rikuchū	
14 Nagato	39 Yamato	53 Etchū	70 Mutsu	
15 Suwō		54 Echigo		
16 Aki		55 Sado	71 Matsumae——Hokkaidō	
17 Iwami Chūgoku				
18 Bingo region				
19 Izumo				
20 Bitchū				
21 Hōki				
22 Mimasaka				
23 Bizen				
24 Inaba				

■ Edo (Tokyo)

Low

Medium low

Medium high

High

Figure 10. Total magnitude of conflict, 1590–1877

Shinano, a significant part of the Kinai, the central section of the Chūgoku, and two provinces in Shikoku. Characteristic of those provinces are vulnerability of provincial agricultural sectors to natural conditions coinciding with high rates of growth in both agricultural productivity and protoindustrial development between 1700 and 1880.[9] Economic growth in an unstable context, rather than poverty, may conduce to contention.

Second, the dimensions of conflict are at the same time separate phenomena and are in some cases found in quite differing magnitudes in different places. The sharpest contrasts are between social and political conflict, on the one hand, and political protest on the other. Provinces ranking high in social and political conflict but low in protest include Musashi, Sagami, and Shimotsuke in the Kantō; Izu and Kai adjoining the Kantō; Etchū and Noto on the Japan Sea coast; and Settsu and Yamashiro in the Kinai. The contrasting group of provinces includes Ugo in the northeast, Mikawa in central Japan, and a set of western provinces: Awaji and Awa, Tango, Mimasaka, Inaba, Hōki, Suō, and Hyūga. I have suggested elsewhere (White 1989) that the relative salience of social conflict in the total varies with the extent of economic advancement of a region; this view is consistent with the present data, with social conflict being characteristic of the Kantō and Kinai and their neighbors, and political protest still overshadowing social conflict in the less economically developed northeast and southwest. The general economic characteristics of provinces available in our data set are of little help in differentiating degree of social conflict and political protest. Two political characteristics, however, do appear influential: provinces ruled in large part by the shōgunal government or bakufu and those highly fragmented among different types of feudal jurisdictions are high in social and political conflict but not noteworthy in degree of political protest.[10] People in loosely governed territories thus seem to enjoy opportunities for contending with their fellow commoners with relative impunity. The anomalous absence of relationship between political control and political protest, however, is a question to be put off to another analysis.

Third, calculating conflict while adjusting for provincial size provides an overview of contention in Tokugawa Japan somewhat at odds with other similar depictions. The Tōhoku is usually seen as the center of collective action; although its provinces rank relatively high,[11] only Rikuchū is in the top category. The real core of contention is the Chūbu region, followed closely by the central Chūgoku and the Iyo–Awa belt across Shikoku. Most surprising, perhaps, is the appearance of Settsu, Izumi, and Kawachi in this group, accompanied by neighboring Tamba and followed closely by Yamashiro and Yamato. Stereotypically, this region has been classified as the best-off in the country economically and the least conflict-prone; adjustment for the small size of these provinces catapults them into the very top rank of contentious areas. Such a revelation should come as sweet vindication to Marxist Japanese scholars who have posited class differentiation as a major source of popular contention and therefore asserted in the face of all (unadjusted) data that there must have been in fact a high level of at least latent conflict potential in the Kinai. Until now such protestations seemed like wishful thinking driven by ideological commitment, but our analysis indicates that, for their size, these provinces were indeed quite conflict-ridden, and the singular salience of social conflict in Settsu and Yamashiro (and the greater, though less discrepant, magnitude of social conflict than protest in Izumi and Kawachi as well) is quite consistent with the hypothesis that class differentiation will conduce more toward intra- than interclass conflict.

However, conventional wisdom makes a reasonable showing when one looks at changes in provincial magnitudes of conflict over time. As Figure 11 shows, conflict increased most in the north and east, including most of the Tōhoku and Kantō.[12] Two provinces in remote Kyūshū saw major increases, but for the most part southern and western Japan saw only minor growth in contention during this period. The Kinai appears to have been quite a contentious region by the beginning of the eighteenth century, as were Shikoku and the Chūgoku. Only in the latter half of the Tokugawa era did the Tōhoku approximate its reputation as the heartland of peasant rebellion. Overall, the pace of economic development may be related to changes in magnitude of contention, since western Japan was already relatively well developed by 1700, and the pace of economic change was considerably quicker in the east in the eighteenth and nineteenth centuries. Such a sweeping statement will bear close scrutiny, since demography—among other factors—also changed during these years, but it is one hypothesis that derives initially from the data.

As the longitudinal comparison of provinces shows, our interest in the distribution of contention is not only spatial but temporal, and an overview of change in contention over time requires attention not only to the quantitative distribution of conflict but also to its qualitative composition. Figure 12 presents data on the total magnitude of conflict for the period under examination, with a logarithmic transformation serving to dampen extreme fluctuations. As the figure shows, the period witnessed a gradual increase in the magnitude of contention, although the trend was also marked by extreme fluctuation and highlighted by two periods of intense conflict—the 1780s and 1830s—and secondary peaks in the latter halves of the 1740s and 1760s and the first halves of the 1810s and 1820s. Like the provincial picture, this one implies one clear hypothesis:

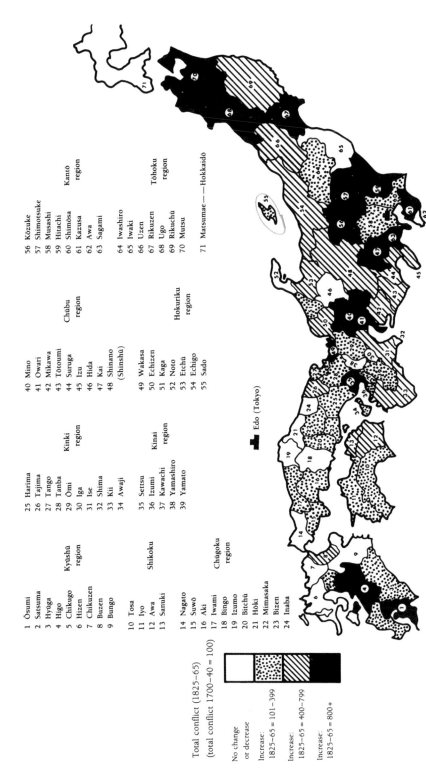

1 Ōsumi	25 Harima	40 Mino	56 Kōzuke	
2 Satsuma	26 Tajima	41 Owari	57 Shimotsuke	
3 Hyūga	27 Tango	42 Mikawa	58 Musashi	
4 Higo	28 Tanba	43 Tōtoumi	59 Hitachi	
5 Chikugo	29 Ōmi	44 Suruga	60 Shimōsa	Kantō
6 Hizen	30 Iga	Kinki	45 Izu	61 Kazusa	region
7 Chikuzen	31 Ise	region	46 Hida	62 Awa	
8 Buzen	32 Shima	47 Kai	63 Sagami	
9 Bungo	33 Kii	48 Shinano		
	34 Awaji	(Shinshū)	64 Iwashiro	
			65 Iwaki	
10 Tosa	35 Settsu	49 Wakasa	66 Uzen	
11 Iyo	36 Izumi	50 Echizen	67 Rikuzen	Tōhoku
12 Awa	Shikoku	37 Kawachi	Kinai	51 Kaga	68 Ugo	region
13 Sanuki	38 Yamashiro	region	52 Noto	69 Rikuchū	
	39 Yamato	53 Etchū	Chūbu	70 Mutsu	
14 Nagato		54 Echigo	region		
15 Suwō		55 Sado	Hokuriku	71 Matsumae —— Hokkaidō	
16 Aki			region		
17 Iwami				
18 Bingo				
19 Izumo				
20 Bitchū	Chūgoku			
21 Hōki	region			
22 Mimasaka				
23 Bizen				
24 Inaba				

🔲 Edo (Tokyo)

Total conflict (1825–65)

(total conflict 1700–40 = 100)

No change
or decrease

Increase:
1825–65 = 101–399

Increase:
1825–65 = 400–799

Increase:
1825–65 = 800+

Figure 11.   Change in total magnitude of conflict, 1700–1740 vs. 1825–1865 (source: Table 3)

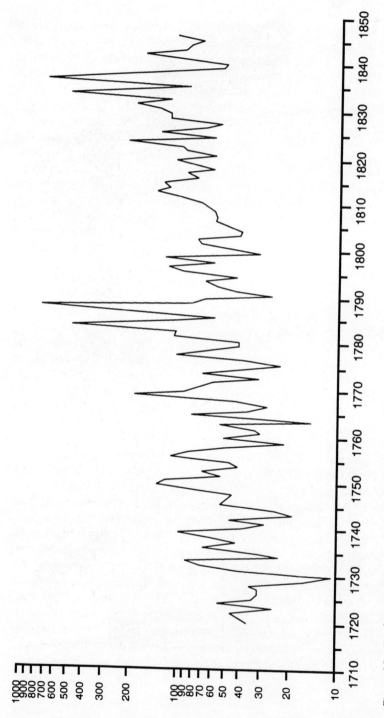

Figure 12. Total magnitude of conflict in Japan, 1720–1846

a link between the Temmei and Tempō famines (and simultaneous periods of political reform) and popular contention. And indeed, those years witnessing high levels of conflict tended slightly to be years in which high numbers of provinces were affected by natural disaster, although the relationship was stronger between conflict levels in a given year and (a) number of disaster-racked provinces in the *previous* year, and (b) the total number of disasters occurring nationwide during that year *plus* the previous four. Also unsurprisingly, conflict of all types was significantly related to the four-city mean price of rice; in this case, however, the connection is strongest in the same year, without any time lags. Moreover, conflict of all types was relatively frequent in years when the bakufu was running financial deficits and imposing relatively low levels of taxation in its territories.[13] The suggestion emerging is that widespread disaster results the following year in high prices and conflict, especially in a context of low bakufu capacity to extract the resources necessary to run an effective government.

Quantitative change is not the only aspect of collective action in which we are interested. Figure 13, therefore, shows the change in the composition of the total magnitude of contention in the years of interest.[14] Litigation and petition, although frequent, never account for more than a trace of the total; political conflict, too, is a minor and relatively consistent category. The major relationship is between social conflict and political protest, and over time the former increases at the proportional expense of the latter (especially if one adds political conflict to social, which is intuitively tempting). From half or more of the total in the first half of the eighteenth century, political protest shrinks to less than 30 percent in the first half of the nineteenth. Equally clear is the relationship between composition and total magnitude of conflict: from the 1880s on, the peaks of contention are driven by upsurges in the proportion of social conflict—they do not represent massive waves of political dissent but rather contention among the common people themselves. Political protest also increased during these peaks, but it was overshadowed by the movements of popular social contention. Perhaps an increasingly debilitated bakufu and its vassals became simply less relevant to the lives of the people in either its perceived causal role in their dissatisfactions or its potential remedial role. The picture here is consistent with the hypothesis that economic development in the eighteenth century created new, increasingly differentiated, and at least potentially incompatible class and stratal formations, interests, resources, and associational patterns within the commoner class and that these developments in turn go far to explain the gradual increase in conflict visible during the period.

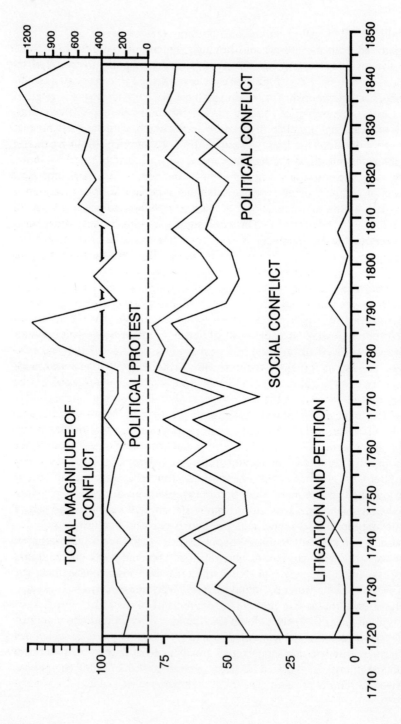

Figure 13. The composition of sociopolitical conflict in Japan, 1720–1846

The Evolution of Contention

Figure 13 indicates some of the ways in which patterns of popular conflict evolved during the later Tokugawa period. Our overview of the phenomenon will conclude with a few additional comments on this score.[15] First, we have noted the increase in both number of incidents and total magnitude of conflict—from only 5 incidents on the average per year during the first half of the seventeenth century to almost 60 annually during the last fifty years of the Tokugawa era (Aoki K., 1981). Second, magnitude rose more dramatically than the number of incidents, reflecting a trend toward bigger, more aggressive, and more organized forms of conflict. Political *gōso* and social *uchikowashi* both increased in number relative to other types of action, although to some extent the increase in scale reflects the relative growth of social conflict, since throughout the era political protest tended to be deferential even when large, and social conflict tended to be more aggressive even when small. Third, as we have also seen, contention became increasingly a social phenomenon. As the Tokugawa government became less of a controlling factor, the reasons for and objectives of contention tended to become less political and more social and economic. The typical confrontation occurred less often between village elites (representing their "constituents") and the government and more often between better-off commoners (e.g., merchants, creditors, and landlords) and others within villages (Yokoyama 1977; Hayashi 1976; Aoki K. 1966; Aoki M. 1981: vols. 1, 2; Rekishigaku Kenkyū Kai 1975; Fukaya 1979).

The Tokugawa era opened with frequent flight by disgruntled peasants and with large scale insurrections, often directed against the imposition of Tokugawa rule. As the seventeenth century wore on, both types faded, and orderly petitions and equally peaceable (albeit illegal) *osso* by village representatives, approaching a now well-established regime, increased. By the eighteenth century bakufu and domain budgetary problems spurred greater efforts at extraction, both through taxation and official trade monopolies, and peasant resistance grew in intensity (with *gōso* becoming prominent) and scope (as peasants faced increasingly common threats nationwide, cross-domain protest grew). The late eighteenth century saw another wave of fiscal reform, the Temmei disasters, and another resultant wave of contention, including unprecedented numbers of food and other urban riots.

The nineteenth century, including the first years of the Meiji era, were characterized by *gōso*, *uchikowashi*, and myriad village disputes as the peasantry had become too fragmented to present a united front to the feudal authorities. The 1830s were characterized by another cycle of disaster-famine-conflict-reform–more conflict, and the pitch of collective action reached hew heights during the economic and political chaos following the opening of Japan to foreign intercourse in the 1850s—but this takes us beyond the scope of this essay.

Summary: Demography and Dissent

Thus far we have undertaken overviews of demographic and conflict phenomena in Japan during the eighteenth and nineteenth centuries. The first aspect of population we looked at was size, and we suggested that it might be expected to be directly related to conflict. Comparison of this idea with our Japanese data, however, leads us to question this proposition. In the first place, on the national level Japan's population grew some 200 to 300 percent during the seventeenth century, almost not at all during the eighteenth, and perhaps 20 to 30 percent during the nineteenth (until the 1870s). Conflict, on the contrary, increased less than 20 percent from the first quarter of the seventeenth century to the last.[16] From the first quarter of the eighteenth century to the last the increase was 288 percent if all years are included, and still 134 percent if the extraordinarily high-conflict years of 1783, 1786, and 1787 are excluded. In the nineteenth century the increase (1801–2185 vs. 1853–1877) was 134 percent if all years are included, and 48 percent if the exceptional highs of 1823, 1858, and 1866–1871 are excluded. Clearly, little can be traced between the rates of change in size of overall population and magnitude of overall conflict.

A second caveat comes from Japanese scholars, who tend to the view that poverty leads to depopulation and also to high levels of conflict: they hypothesize not only an inverse relationship, but a spurious one as well. And finally, a glance back at Table 3 indicates inconsistencies between data and theory. The provinces evincing the greatest increases in total magnitude of conflict between the years 1721 and 1846 include much of the Kantō and Kinki, which declined in population, but also such areas as Kai, Shinano, Hida, and Iwami, which grew. Thus size in and of itself may have little to do with levels of conflict. Our initial hypothesis is not definitively disconfirmed as yet, but we shall entertain suspicions as we take a closer look at the relationships between size and conflict.

Similar suspicions shall accompany our examination of the relationship between density and conflict. As noted, density is often associated with conflict but ordinarily in tacit or overt combination with food supply, by which it becomes converted into population pressure.[17] Density may be highly relevant as an indicator of urbanism, but here too it loses much of its intrinsic utility.

Population pressure has been perhaps our most-used concept thus far. Initially we expected that high and increasing density would be associated with higher levels of conflict; in the Japanese context this relationship seemed to take on special interest if reconceived not as the result of increasing population and a static food supply but as that of a constant population—particularly a nonagrarian population vulnerable to markets for both the food it bought and the goods it sold—and a suddenly decreased food supply reduced by natural disaster. The work of Japanese scholars reinforces this expectation, but our overview of population and demographic data confound it. Specifically, when one compares the data on change in agricultural productivity of Japan's provinces between roughly 1700 and 1880 (Nakamura 1968:175, 183) with the data in Table 3, one discovers that increased conflict during the period is associated with *decreasing* population pressure. The top 14 provinces in terms of increased agricultural productivity and the bottom 14 were selected and the extent of change in their populations and levels of conflict were compared, with the single most egregious outlier excluded from each group (which makes the initial contrast a bit sharper). Those whose productivity increased *most* had a mean population index of 100 in 1721 and still 100 in 1846; their average conflict index went from 100 to 640. The *least*-increase provinces went from a population index of 100 to 115; their average conflict index went from 100 to 257. In other words, our crude preliminary analysis suggests that higher levels of conflict were associated with both absolute and per capita increases in the food supply, i.e., decreasing pressure.[18] This analysis says nothing about absolute levels of conflict, but it forces reconsideration of the ideas derived from previous theory. It also dovetails with the data presented by Saitō Osamu (1985:217) that show high levels of cereal production in the high-conflict regions of western Japan.

This reconsideration points us toward resource- or opportunity-based notions of conflict (Oberschall 1973; Tilly 1978). According to this approach, it is not increasing pressure (and by implication increasing need and dearth) but increasing "elbow room" in terms of a margin above and beyond subsistence that contributes to conflict in societies in which oppression and exploitation are constants. The poorest and those becoming more and more poor are less likely to protest than those who have some extra resources beyond subsistence with which to act and enough time to take off from food-producing activities to make political behavior possible. This approach comes close to turning the density thesis on its head, although in actuality it does so only over the long run; it is in no way incompatible with short-term protest among the relatively better-off when their prosperity is threatened by extraordinary market or

crop fluctuations.[19] Indeed, it is a sensible corrective to the easy inference from Hanley and Yamamura (1977) that the increasing agricultural
productivity and elevated standards of living of the Japanese countryside
in the eighteenth and nineteenth centuries should lead to diminished
levels of conflict among an increasingly satisfied populace (Kelly
1985:15ff.). Prosperity might mask increasingly unequal division of its
own fruits; it might portend the multiplication and heterogenization of
potentially contradictory economic interests; it might be based on new
forms of exploitation; and it might be uneven across regions (White
1989; Kelly 1985). It might also be the ironic result of earlier misery: it
is possible that the poorest areas of the country were (for that reason)
susceptible to conflict and also to poverty-push out-migration; sufficient
out-migration would increase the per-capita food supply, which in turn
(according to the resource-mobilization approach) also contributes to
higher levels of conflict.

   Thus conflict could come both directly from poverty and indirectly,
through out-migration and increased food for those remaining (White
1981). It is also possible that diminished pressure on the food supply
has different effects in city and country: perhaps the resource-
mobilization model would suggest an inverse relationship in the countryside where food resources are produced, whereas a density-conflict model
would better explain conflict in the city, where vulnerable populations
respond to diminished pressure with quiescence.[20] And finally, decreased
population pressure, as an index of economic development, may be
indirectly linked to contention through the agency of politics: as Jack
Goldstone has argued (personal communication, November 1988), either
protoindustrially or agriculturally based economic development (either or
both of which are, as Saitō [1985:215–217] shows, high in high-conflict
regions) led to lower prices for rice. Bakufu and domain taxes were col-
lected or denominated in terms of rice. Thus economic development led
to decreased revenues and, by inference, to the sorts of administrative
weakness I have shown elsewhere (White 1988d) to be associated with
increased opportunities to challenge the authorities. Moreover, the standard measures taken to remedy this revenue reduction—increased tax
rates, regulation or taxation of commerce and protoindustry, and
currency debasement—all provoked popular resistance. And the governments *most* likely to take such provocative steps were precisely those
being starved fiscally and thus emasculated in their coercive capabilities.
The complexity of the problem is clear, and careful analysis is in order.

   The question of population distribution has thus far had three aspects:
distribution as *rate* of urbanization, as *level* of urbanism, and as *concentration* of migrants. Contemporary observers focused on the last: the

migrant poor were continually decried (and relieved) by the Tokugawa authorities (Minami 1978). But in fact the most conflict-ridden years of the Tokugawa city were its last, when in-migration was decreasing, and what documentation exists suggests that migrants often constituted a minority of the population of the poorer section of the cities from whence conflict arose (White 1981:20ff.) and that riot participants were not rootless newcomers but those relatively well established (Kajinishi 1978:92ff.). Migrants might well have been overrepresented in urban conflict, but there is little reason to expect them to have pre-dominated.

Urbanization, as rate of change, also gets little support from prior research as a factor in high magnitudes of conflict, although we might well expect high levels of urbanism to be related thereto. This expectation is supported by our Japanese data, at this provisional point, for much of the Tokugawa period. Between 1590 and 1720—when Japan's cities were rapidly growing—specifically urban forms of conflict accounted for 7 percent of total conflict; between 1721 and 1770 the proportion was 16 percent; between 1771 and 1820, 24 percent; between 1821 and 1846, 22 percent—and in all three of these later periods the rate of urbanization was essentially zero. Between 1771 and 1846 cities were clearly overrepresented as arenas of conflict, given Aoki's narrow definition of urban conflict and his focus on the larger towns and cities (one will recall that the proportion of the population in towns over 10,000 was only some 12 or 13 percent [Jansen and Rozman 1986:323]). In other words, once the process of urbanization was largely complete, conflict moved cityward, particularly social conflict. As we saw from figures 6 through 10, social conflict was relatively salient in the urban Kantō and Kinki, whereas political protest was relatively salient in the more rural Tōhoku and southwest. In any case, we might expect to find more conflict in the more urban areas of Japan during the bulk of the period. Such a relationship, however, is not neatly linear: it is not the central cores of such metropolitan areas as Edo and Ōsaka but the counties on their immediate peripheries that saw the most contention.

Finally, we come to the subject of natural disaster, and here an unaccustomed and blissful consensus characterizes both prior research and our preliminary look at the Aoki data. Conflict flourished during dearth, and most such periods were caused by natural catastrophe, not simply market distortion or fluctuation, although they were exacerbated by governmental inflexibility and decay. In the Kyōhō period political reform—specifically a set of rice-price support policies that unfortunately coincided with a plague of locusts—immediately preceded a wave of conflict; in the Temmei and Tempō periods the relationship went the

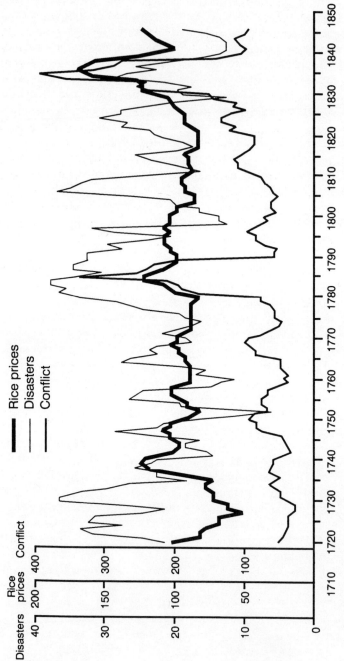

Figure 14. Fluctuations in natural disasters, rice prices, and sociopolitical conflict, 1720–1846.
Disasters: Number of provinces annually affected by disaster, five-year floating average (source: Arakawa 1964:248–262)
Rice price: Four-city mean annual rice price, five-year floating average (1840–1844 = 100) (source: see Figure 4)
Conflict: Total magnitude of all forms of conflict, five-year floating average.

other way: natural disaster led to conflict, which led to reform (Arakawa 1967:61; Yamada 1984:204ff.; Sasaki J. 1974:297ff.). The relationship between disaster and conflict, mediated by the price of rice as shown in Figure 14, is a consistent one, especially after the 1730s. The relationship is not an immediate one: the price of rice is closely correlated to levels of conflict, but number of provinces affected by disaster is related to both with a one-year time lag. As Harada Tomohiko (1982:385) has noted, temporary despair was less likely to lead directly to conflict than cumulative despair. And a composite measure (the product of rice price times disaster-affected provinces in the previous year) is correlated to conflict (all forms except petition) at between $r = .46$ and $r = .52$. We must still attempt to assess the differential effect of rice prices on rural (i.e., producer population) and urban (i.e., consumer population) areas, but there is enough evidence thus far to support our hypothesis that disaster contributes to conflict through the agency of intensified population pressure on the food supply.

THREE

Demography and Dissidence:
A Quantitative Analysis

Armed with the expectations discussed in the previous chapter, let us now see if our data on population and popular contention prove useful in clarifying the relationships in which we are interested. Most of these data are, as noted, provincial-level (although we shall bring in our time-series data also at times); we shall look first at them all together, considering Japan as a whole. Aware that there are other meaningful ways to disaggregate the nation, such as into regions or into more or less urban or more or less climatically capricious areas, we shall also regroup our provinces and look at them as such. But first, let us assess our five dimensions of population on the national level.

The National Level
Size

We have measured the size of provincial population in four ways: large or small in both the eighteenth and nineteenth centuries, and growing or declining in each century.[1] Absolute population size we find to be modestly related to *per koku* levels of petition and litigation, social conflict, and political conflict in both centuries, with correlation coefficients (Pearson r) ranging from .14 to .41. Political protest, however, showed no significant relationship in either century. This finding was unexpected. The largest provinces—Mutsu and Dewa in the north, Yamashiro (home of Kyōto), Settsu (home of Ōsaka), and Musashi (home of Edo)—were among the more contentious provinces, for reasons that may well have nothing to do with their intrinsic size.

Change in population size bore no consistent and significant relationship to any form of conflict. Magnitudes of provincial change ranged from –50 percent to +60 percent in the eighteenth century, and between -17 percent and +100 percent in the nineteenth, so that lack of variation does not appear to be the reason. For whatever reason, neither the general theoretical expectation (population growth conduces to conflict) nor the distinctively Japanese expectation (poverty leads to population decrease and to conflict, creating a spurious negative association between growth and contention) is supported.

Density

In measuring population density we used two different indices. The first was simple density of people per square kilometer of provincial territory; the second was density per unit of arable land in the province. Densities were calculated for both eighteenth and nineteenth centuries for each type of density; changes in density were also calculated for each century for each type of density.[2] The analysis, however, was a total washout—as hypothesized, density per se (as opposed to density of certain types, e.g., urbanization, or vis-à-vis other factors such as food supply) counts for nothing. Our measure of density on cultivable land might have approximated a measure of population pressure on the food supply, but if so there is nothing here either.

Pressure

In order to get at the notion of population pressure, I used a variety of measures, that data from other societies indicate will be related positively to conflict (although our sketchy overview of some Japanese data indicates quite the opposite). The first index was gross and net (after taxes) agricultural productivity per capita in both the eighteenth and nineteenth centuries, and changes therein from the beginning of the eighteenth to the middle of the nineteenth century.[3] The second was gross and net calories of food production per capita during the Edo period.[4] The third was the change in agricultural productivity relative to population change during the Edo period.[5]

Overall, analysis supported the suggestions of the Japanese data that greater pressure on the food supply is related to lower levels of conflict, not higher. The relationships found were hardly universal—food supply in terms of calories per capita, for example, showed no tie whatsoever and changes in gross and net *kokudaka* per capita during the eighteenth and nineteenth centuries showed only suggestions—albeit significant ones: correlation coefficients ran in the .20 to .30 range. Again, political protest was almost entirely unaffected by these factors. But, repeatedly, modest links between higher pressure and lower levels of the other forms of conflict emerged. Again, it is possible that spurious relationships exist: perhaps the poorest provinces were depopulating (and thus declining in population pressure, assuming that the lower population could maintain prior levels of food production) and also giving rise to more conflict. The problem here is that the more socially contentious (and also depopulating) provinces included highly urban Musashi and Settsu-Kawachi-Izumi, hardly poverty-stricken areas. In these regions it is possible that certain urban qualities led both to demographic stagnation and, independently, to contention. It may be that different patterns characterize less urban and more urban centers of contention, a question to which we shall turn later.

Urbanism and Urbanization

Very little urban growth, or urbanization, took place during the period at which we are looking; the era of urbanization in Tokugawa Japan was the seventeenth century. Thus one expects little in the way of a relationship between urbanization and conflict. But contention did urbanize: the seventeenth-century underrepresentation of cities in the panoply of conflict gave way in later years to overrepresentation. Moreover, the urban Kinai and Kantō ranked among the most contentious regions in Japan. At the same time, however, the much less urban Chūbu and Hokuriku saw some of the highest levels of social conflict, and the even more peripheral parts of Shikoku, Kyūshū, and western Honshū witnessed high levels of political protest. Aggregating to the national level might not be the wisest analytical step to take, but it can certainly be the first.

We have only one measure of urbanism, and it is as rough as most of our other measures.[6] On the national level, we found urbanism to be modestly related to social and political conflict ($r = .18$, $r = .33$) and nonsignificantly related to petition and litigation as well ($r = .10$), but not related to political protest at all. The independent explanatory power of a factor showing associations such as these is close to nil, and we are not encouraged by the knowledge that, *within* the most urban provinces, it is the peripheral counties, not the metropolitan core, that were the most contentious.

Disaster

The last of the aspects of population of interest to us here is crisis; its surrogate here is natural disaster. We have already found that natural disaster, acting hypothetically through the agency of higher food prices, is positively related to conflict across time. Are chronically disaster-prone regions also typified by higher levels of contention?

We have only one measure of disaster-proneness, and (like urbanism) it is a measure that applies to the entire Edo period, not to each century (see Chapter 2, note 2), and is thus correlated to aggregate measures of conflict for the entire period, not for each century. The correlations found are weak but in the predicted direction, at least for social conflict ($r = .18$) and petition and litigation ($r = .30$). Political protest, on the contrary, seems to be negatively associated with calamity ($r = -.21$), albeit equally weakly. This is perhaps unsurprising, given the relative salience of protest among the different types of conflict in southern and western Japan. But it does complicate the picture in ways we should investigate further.

Disaggregating the Picture

At this point we might be either disappointed or satisfied. Disappointment might derive from the modesty of our results thus far: we have found little relevance in some of our demographic variables, with several washing out altogether and none explaining more than 15 percent of the variance in any type of conflict (indeed, most accounted for 6 to 10 percent). We might be engaged in is a substantial exercise in confirming a null hypothesis. Such an exercise is in no way scientifically unworthy—indeed, it would support many of the findings recounted above that indicate that demographic conditions and changes are at best indirect, distant, and modest influences on collective behavior. Moreover, it would refute some of the more simplistic eco-apocalyptic assertions about, for example, population pressure and conflict.

But we must question these findings. Perhaps they represent empirically weak relationships, especially in the case of political protest. A second possibility is that they are the result of poor data. Our conflict data have demonstrated some utility elsewhere (White 1988a, 1989, 1988d), but these and our other data are old, imprecise, and full of measurement error—some of them are taken from the 1870s and extrapolated back through the entire period at which we are looking. I have tried to reduce error by recoding all of our variables into quartiles—thus, although it is hardly likely that two provinces with recorded populations of 630,000 and 640,000 were in fact 10,000 people apart, it is also unlikely that they were in fact so far apart (by virtue of error) that they would not be in the same quartile of approximately 18 provinces. I have also, in the case of our era-long but post facto data, tried to limit them to factors (like urbanism) that were unlikely to change dramatically during the era. But the possibility of poor data remains.

A third possibility is that we have not used the right variables; in particular, perhaps some combination of those variables having thus far indicated some utility would contribute more to our understanding than each taken in isolation. And finally, perhaps the gross level of aggregation at which we have been working explains our findings. Those who have found little or no relationship between population and conflict (Gurr 1970; Gurr and Weil 1973; Hibbs 1973; Sanders 1981) have worked at even grosser levels, aggregating dozens of nations and aiming toward the most macro-level analysis of the micro-level relationship between individuals and their environments. In Japan in particular, it is common to disaggregate the country into east and west or into even smaller regions with considerable theoretical justification (Hanley and Yamamura 1977; Bowen 1988; Skinner 1987; Saitō 1985). Therefore, before accepting either the null hypothesis across the board or the assumption of poor data, let us carry out first a multivariate and second a disaggregated analysis of the relationships of interest.

A Multivariate Aside

There are two ways one may simultaneously examine the effects of more than one influence on whatever one is trying to explain. The first and more orthodox is straightforward multivariate analysis such as partial correlation or multiple regression. The alternative is to combine the influences of interest into one and examine the relationship between their combined form and the phenomenon to be explained. At this point the second is preferable, simply because such techniques as multiple regression do not appear merited by the modesty of the relationships thus far discerned. Multiple regression would produce results of extraordinary apparent precision but, in all likelihood, very little explanatory power. With modest data, modest methods are called for. Should we discover more imposing relationships later on, we may opt for commensurate techniques.

The chosen composite measure of demographic effect on contention is the simple product of four factors: absolute provincial population (the mean of the eighteenth- and nineteenth-century populations), increase in agricultural productivity relative to population (i.e., declining population pressure), urbanism, and provincial frequency of natural disasters.[7] Our resulting index of demographic conduciveness to conflict is indeed positively related to petition and litigation ($r = .34$), social conflict (.36), and political conflict (.25); again, political protest appears unaffected. Something does appear to be at work here, although what it is may differ in different types of provinces: the eight provinces ranking highest on our composite measure include highly urban Musashi, Yamato, and Settsu; peripheral urban Kōzuke, Yamashiro, and Harima, and peripheral Kii and Mutsu. The nine lowest-ranking provinces are more uniform in nature: Bōsō Awa, Noto, Shima, Tango, Tajima, Hōki, and Oki are all relatively remote from major urban centers, although Izu and Tōtōmi are located along the major national Pacific coast thoroughfare, the Tōkaidō. Nevertheless, disaggregation of such groups of provinces might reveal more than we can see here.

What we can see already, however, is clearly significant. When one compares even these relatively heterogeneous groups of provinces, one finds that the high-ranking group witnessed 30 percent more petition and litigation, 2.8 times more social conflict, and 3.6 times more political conflict than the low-ranking group during the period from 1721 to 1846. (Levels of political protest, again, did not differ across the two groups.) But what does this contrast really mean? One suspects that size comes in spuriously, owing to the presence in this group of Mutsu, Musashi, and Settsu, with their great populations. Decreasing pressure on the food supply could also be spurious—the result of depopulation caused by intense poverty that also caused conflict. Or it might represent an increase of resources in the hands of people who needed only this bit of elbow room above the subsistence line before they could turn their attention from subsistence to the structures of political and mercantile exploitation that affected them daily and were largely responsible for their low positions.

Size may also be a meretricious factor in the lowest-ranking group. All of these nine provinces are coastal (and therefore relatively flat and warm), and none save Awa is in the eastern part of the country. All are relatively rural and free of natural disasters. As for increasing pressure on the food supply, in such a southern and disaster-free context, an increase in pressure may have taken place on a basis of previously (before 1700) relatively high levels of agricultural productivity.

Disaggregation: East and West

Thus far we have seen several indications that data analysis on the national level may mask or distort relationships among the phenomena of interest to us. Several criteria for disaggregating our data from a 70-province unity to multiple smaller groups of provinces have also been suggested. One exercise for which there is considerable precedent is the comparison of eastern and western Japan. A variety of linguistic, economic, and cultural forms vary systematically between east and west. I have divided our provinces in the standard place—roughly around Owari province—and compared the two regions.

In eastern Japan only a few demographic variables are substantially associated with contention, but they point in interesting ways. First, all four forms of conflict (including political protest) vary inversely with population density vis-à-vis total provincial land area in both centuries (the average of eight *r* values is –.34) but directly with density vis-à-vis arable land (with the exception of petition and litigation; the average of six *r* values is .25). Eastern Japan is characterized by contentious provinces with large territories and relatively small populations but also with relatively little arable land. Additionally, conflict here also varies directly with pressure on the food supply in terms of gross and net assessed agricultural production per capita in both centuries (mean of four *r* values is .40).

In western Japan—away from the presumed demographically relevant depopulation and natural disaster—population appears far more relevant. A modest relationship (*r* = .24) between natural disaster and social conflict appears, along with a similarly modest but inverse tie (*r* = –.25) to political protest. Population size in both centuries is positively linked to social and political conflict, whereas growth during the entire era is linked negatively thereto (mean of six *r* values is .30); these two forms of contention as well as petition are also positively linked to density on total provincial territory in both centuries (mean of six *r* values is .27). Conflict of all four forms varies inversely with food supply (i.e., directly with pressure) in all of its forms (mean of 16 *r* values is –.22), with across-the-board relationships to social conflict and petition and litigation (mean of 12 *r* values is –.26). At the same time, however, all forms of contention except protest also vary directly with *increases* in agricultural productivity per capita (i.e., inversely with increases in pressure; mean of six *r* values is .23). In combination, it appears as if conflict tends to occur frequently in contexts of high but decreasing population size and pressure on the food supply, that is, where the agricultural economy indicates overall dearth accompanied by a trend toward improvement or, otherwise put, toward increased opportunities and resources for contention.

Disaggregation: Urban and Rural

The second division of provinces tried involved distinguishing those ranking highest and lowest on our index of urbanism. In the least urban provinces two sets of relationships emerged: social and political conflict varied positively with provincial population size in both centuries (mean of four *r* values is .45), and all four forms of conflict varied inversely with density vis-à-vis total provincial territory in both centuries (mean of 8 *r* values is –.23). Where cities are not a part of the picture, large populations (but small relative to territory) are associated with contention.

Where cities are part of the picture, in our most urban provinces, population in many forms becomes much more relevant to our understanding of conflict. Conflict (except for protest, which varies inversely:

mean $r = -.33$) varies directly with population size in both centuries (mean of four r values is .45), whereas all four forms of conflict vary inversely with population growth across the entire era (mean of four r values is $-.40$): relatively urban provinces whose populations were large but stagnant were the most contentious. Density of all types, in both centuries, was also positively linked to conflict (mean of 16 r values is .39): the more dense the urban areas but the more sparse the rural, the more contentious.

The relationship between pressure on the food supply in the more urban provinces is the same as that found in the western provinces: conflict is higher where there is low but increasing food production per capita, net and gross. Food productivity per capita, in both koku and calories and in both centuries, was inversely related to conflict of all four types at a mean (24 cases) of $r = -.36$, whereas increased productivity was linked to all four types (12 cases) at a mean of $r = .45$. And finally we see a modest ($r = .36$) connection between natural disasters and social conflict, although a similarly modest but inverse relationship ($r = -.24$) appears for political protest.

Disaggregation: Agrarian Vulnerability

The final technique by which we might expect to discover distinctive patterns of demography and dissidence is that of disaggregating our 70 provinces on the basis of the vulnerability of their agricultural sectors to natural disaster. Our measure of vulnerability is simply the product of each province's modal altitude and average annual number of frost-free days, the presumption being that colder mountainous areas will be more vulnerable than warmer lowland ones. The justification for the exercise is equally simple: discussions of depopulation in general and population crisis in particular focus (with the exception of the insect-induced Kyōhō famine in western Japan in the 1730s) almost exclusively on the more mountainous, colder Chūbu and Tōhoku regions.

Focusing first on the more agriculturally viable provinces, we find that—as was the case with western Japan—population factors matter more than expected. Population size (in both centuries) and decrease conduce modestly toward social and political conflict (mean of six r values is .24), and population density vis-à-vis arable land conduces, in both centuries, toward all forms of contention except political conflict (mean of six r values is .24). High pressure on the food supply (as measured by gross and net *kokudaka* per capita in both centuries and gross calories per capita) is related to higher levels of petition and social conflict (mean of ten r values is .29) and, as found before, so is diminishing pressure during the era: petition, social conflict, and political conflict correlate with our two measures of changing agricultural productivity per capita at a mean (of six r values) of .27. Even in this group of provinces, natural disasters contribute positively ($r = .29$), but only to social conflict—the link between disasters and political protest is again negative ($r = -.22$).

Turning to the most vulnerable group of provinces, we find similarly modest, albeit clear and different, patterns. Among these provinces it is those which gained population which saw more social conflict and political protest ($r = .29, .37$). Low density on total provincial territory but high density on arable land is associated here and there in both centuries with all four types of contention (16 possible correlations of which 9 were substantial; mean r of these nine values is .22), especially protest. Low (gross and net) food supplies per capita are positively related to both social conflict and political protest in both centuries (mean of eight r values is .30) and (contrary to what we found elsewhere) diminishing agricultural productivity per capita of both types (i.e., increasing population pressures) are also related positively to political protest (mean of two r values is .31).

What, then, may we say on the basis of this disaggregated analysis of population and popular conflict? First, it may be that those who have found negligible relationships between these phenomena have simply approached the matter on the wrong level. Subnational, not national-level (much less 60-nation aggregate) studies might be the best way to get at what is going on. Second, in contradiction of our earlier national-level findings, something does appear to be going on. Third, it is not going on everywhere to the same degree: demographic factors appear more relevant to the study of conflict in western than eastern Japan, in more rather than less urban provinces, and to a similar extent (albeit in different ways) in provinces with differing degrees of agricultural vulnerability. Fourth, we should ask if this disaggregation—a form of statistical control for region, urbanism, and vulnerability—reveals any common relationships.

The answer to this question is yes, in three ways. First, larger but declining provincial populations are associated with conflict everywhere except in the easternmost and more vulnerable provinces, and in eastern Japan large and increasing populations are consistently, albeit weakly, associated with conflict. It may be that outside the relatively vulnerable east stagnant population reflects either an urban population drain or rural economic stagnation; Table 3 suggests that this is primarily but not exclusively (note Yamato, Ise, Iga, Kii, Mimasaka, Bungo and Ōsumi) the case. It is hard to believe that fewer people per se leads to higher rates of conflict; it is more likely that population size and growth are configurational variables (which connote or imply certain values of certain other variables) rather than causal ones. A configurational quality does not reduce the relevance of population, but it does change its nature.

Second, population density on arable land is generally associated with higher levels of conflict (Hayami 1988:201), although it often is so in tandem with low density on provincial territory as a whole. Large populations in even larger territories (but territories only relatively small proportions of which are arable) appear to be the locus of disproportionate magnitudes of conflict.

Third and intuitively linked to the relevance of density on arable land is the association between population pressure on the food supply and contention; in western, urban, and agriculturally viable provinces contention is associated with decreasing pressure. One might hazard the hypothesis that where the people already have a higher presumptive margin above subsistence (e.g., in Tokugawa Japan's more western, urban, and viable provinces), high but decreasing pressure on the food supply translates into increasing resources in the hands of people who still feel tension between their futures and their food supplies. Such resources might be used to seek further respite from those who might want to separate the people from the increasing fruits of their labor, especially if increased resources in the hands of the people imply fewer resources (and thus coercive and administrative capabilities) in the hands of government. Where such preexisting breathing room does not exist (presumptively, in those more agriculturally vulnerable regions where pressure on the food supply is also high), the complementary hypothesis is that increasing food supplies may simply move people farther from a point at which desperation might make resistance imperative and thus conduce to less rather than more contention.

Fourth, we should note the distinctive role of natural disaster (and, by hypothetical extension, demographic crisis). It has played almost no role at all in our analyses, appearing here and there but always in a minor key and never consistently. Disaster has only one distinctive role in our spatially oriented analysis: it appears to have positive links to social and related conflict, and negative links to political protest. But aside from this role, its relevance appears to be overwhelmingly temporal: the conflictual implications of natural calamity appear to work across provinces at specific times, with impact that washes out provincial differences. The surges of conflict visible in the 1780s and 1830s are unquestionably linked to the crop failures and famines that occurred then, but in this instance it is the nation as a whole, or at least great regions thereof, that is the relevant arena of analysis.

And finally we should note the common nonappearance in all these analyses of a phenomenon of major interest: political protest. It occasionally surfaces, but always in a most minor way and never consistently. In another analytical exercise (White 1989), I have shown that protest is much more weakly linked to economic development in a variety of its manifestations than are social and political conflict and petition and litigation. Here again economically driven models of political behavior prove perhaps less useful than those explicitly focusing on political causes.

The Dimensions of Demography: How Relevant Are They, and How Relevant Is Each?

The above data lead us in two final directions. First, if such factors as population and economics do not significantly help us explain political protest, for example, then what does? And, to what extent do such factors as population help us explain collective action of all types relative to such things as the economy, the polity, and so forth? These questions take us into a realm of analysis and conceptualization far beyond the capacity of this volume to circumscribe, and we shall simply pass them by.

The second direction is simpler: let us attempt to measure the relative impact on collective contention of each of the dimensions of population discussed above. On the national level we attempted only—by means of our composite measure of demographic conduciveness—to evaluate the overall relevance of a group of demographic variables to conflict. But on the subnational level we have discovered a variety of relationships of sufficient significance to merit more ambitious analysis, and therefore I shall conclude this exercise with a comparative analysis, at our three disaggregated subnational levels, of the different aspects of population sketched out above.

The technique we shall adopt is multiple regression. This technique enables us to do two things: first, we can measure the independent effect of each dimension of population on each form of conflict when all the other dimensions are held constant by calculating for each dimension a statistic called a "standardized regression coefficient" or "beta." Second, we can combine all of the dimensions at once and see (a) how strongly all of them taken together are related to conflict (shown by the "multiple correlation coefficient" or R) and (b) how much of the variation in each form of conflict is accounted for by all of them together, that is, by population in all of its manifestations incorporated here (the R^2). We cannot, of course, determine the relevance of all these aspects of population, taken together, relative to economic and political factors and so forth. Nor can we fill in the blanks in our analysis with methodological sleight-of-hand. Between demographic and behavioral phenomena stand at least two intervening factors: a mixture of social, cultural, political, and economic structures and individual attitudes. Thus any real attempt at explaining the relevance of population to contention requires interpolation between demographic conditions and behavioral ones. In a future exercise I hope to insert some of these intervening phenomena. But even now we may still be able to make some exploratory statements regarding the overall relevance of a population focus in studies of collective action.[8]

First, on the basis of the foregoing analysis, eight variables were selected for their potential: one measure of population size (provincial population in the nineteenth century), two measures of density (vis-à-vis total land and arable land in the nineteenth century), two of static population pressure (productivity in calories per capita and gross *kokudaka* per capita in the nineteenth century), and one of dynamic pressure (change in agricultural productivity relative to population), plus our measures of urbanism and natural disaster. A number of other measures that have played a significant role thus far (in particular, the eighteenth-century versions of several of the above and the net versions of some) were too closely associated with others (or "multicollinear") to permit their inclusion. Where multicollinearity was a problem, I kept only those variables showing the stronger relationships to conflict in our prior analysis. Another variable that I eliminated was population change during the entire era, which was strongly correlated with almost every other one of our explanatory variables. This situation strengthens the suspicion that population size is more of a configurational than an explanatory variable: many things are associated with it, but probably few are influenced by it. Finally, there were instances of potential multicollinearity in specific subsets of provinces, and in such cases one or two more variables were culled; thus the final analyses included between six and eight independent variables.

Table 6 presents the results of the regression and permits several observations. The overall relevance of our demographic phenomena is modest but clear: in 24 analyses, population played a meaningful explanatory role in 13. The forms of conflict most explicable by population are social conflict (mean of four R^2 values is 40 percent), political conflict (mean = 25 percent), and petition and litigation (mean = 16 percent). In terms of provincial categories, population appears most relevant in eastern Japan (mean of three R^2 values is 45 percent), followed by western (16 percent) and more agriculturally viable (20 percent) provinces. Although only two forms of conflict were demo-graphically explained there, the explanatory power of population was considerable in urban provinces also (mean = 52 percent). Protest was, as we have seen repeatedly, minimally explicable by population factors, as was conflict in general in both more rural and more agriculturally vulnerable provinces.

Beyond the low relevance of population to protest and in vulnerable provinces, no specific findings can be emphasized with great confidence. However, four broad conclusions can be drawn. First, when other aspects of population are controlled for, size per se fades in importance, appearing only once in Table 6. This finding is not surprising.[9] The second conclusion, however, is: natural disaster fades also, despite its relevance as a temporally distributed phenomenon. Third, more surpris-ing still, population distribution (i.e., urbanism) fades as an independent explanatory factor, although clearly different patterns of correlation may be discerned between more rural and more urban provinces. And fourth, population pressure—especially vis-à-vis the food supply—emerges as the most significant aspect of population: it is a factor in 11 of the 13 meaningful results presented. In 5 analyses high pressure alone explained substantial variation in magnitude of conflict; in 3 cases decreasing pres-sure alone mattered; and in 3 instances we see again a combination of high but decreasing pressure associated with high levels of popular con-tention. Again, decreasing pressure appears to matter most in the more urban, viable, and western provinces (although it appears also in regard to protest in eastern Japan).

Thus our analysis has indicated that population is more relevant to the study of collective contention than many studies have concluded, albeit less relevant than considerable impressionistic conventional wis-dom presumes. It may fade when empirical data are used to fill the inferential gaps noted above, but at this analytical stage it appears to be quite relevant. Indeed, demographic factors account for over half of the variance in some forms of contention in certain subsets of provinces. In the case of Tokugawa Japan population matters in a variety of ways. In eastern Japan and in relatively rural provinces, population size and stag-nation are relatively significant but, in all likelihood, mainly because the east is dominated by the two old provinces of Mutsu and Dewa and is also the location of Kōzuke and Shimotsuke, the two provinces of most precipitous population decline during the era, and Musashi, the country's clearest case of metropolitan population drain.

Elsewhere in Japan it is difficult to avoid the suspicion that, in the areas of social conflict—including instances in which such conflict led to political action—and such legal remonstrance as petition and litigation,

Table 6

Population and Contention in Japan's Provinces

| | | Type of Conflict | | |
Provincial Category	Petition and Litigation	Social Conflict	Political Conflict	Political Protest
1. Eastern provinces	Natural disaster: .49 $R = .49, R^2 = 24\%$	*Kokudaka* per capita: −.69; Density on all land: −.56 $R = .73, R^2 = 54\%$	none	Density on all land: −.73 Calories per capita: −.56 Increase in agri. prod: .38 $R = .76, R^2 = 58\%$
Western provinces	*Kokudaka* per cap.: −.34 $R = .34, R^2 = 12\%$	*Kokudaka* per cap.: −.44 Increase in agri. prod.: .34 $R = .50, R^2 = 25\%$	Increase in agri. prod: .34 $R = .34, R^2 = 12\%$	none

2. Rural provinces	*Kokudaka* per cap.: -.38 $R = .38, R^2 = 15\%$	none	Population in 19th c.: .42 $R = .42, R^2 = 17\%$	none
Urban provinces	none	Increase in agri. prod: .71 $R = .73, R^2 = 54\%$	Calories per capita: -.73 $R = .71, R^2 = 50\%$	none
3. Agriculturally viable provinces	*Kokudaka* per capita: -.36 $R = .36, R^2 = 13\%$	*Kokudaka* per capita: -.48 Increase in agri. prod.: .39 $R = .57, R^2 = 32\%$	Increase in agri. prod: .40 $R = .40, R^2 = 16\%$	none
Agriculturally vulnerable provinces	none	none	none	none

NOTE: Only those variables that fulfilled the criteria for inclusion in the SPSS multiple regression program using forward data entry (SPSS 1983:ch. 33; Norusis 1985:54–55) appear here; both betas and multiple R values are statistically significant. In cases marked "none," none of the variables in the equation contributed significantly and independently to the variance in the dependent variable.

people were more likely to act collectively where there was a high but frequently decreasing degree of demographic pressure on the food supply, owing either to moderate population size and low economic base (as in the east) or to a substantial economic base combined with a large population (as in the west). This pressure does not appear to be the result of rapacious taxation but rather the availability and productivity of the land relative to the people on it. In fact, it is suggested here that it is pressure—the number of agriculturally unproductive native *or* migrant mouths to feed—and not the innate qualities of cities or migrants (both much maligned) that account for the correlation of contention with urbanism in Tokugawa Japan. Scarcity of resources in city or country may well increase the probability of friction regarding their allocation, especially if this allocation occurs in a context where immediate subsistence is not chronically (or is even decreasingly) threatened. In other words, those who associate contention with a *condition* of poverty, near subsistence, or vulnerable standards of living appear to be right; those who associate it with a long-term *process* of increasing immiseration appear diametrically wrong. And the concepts of poverty and vulnerability must be separated: the demographic stagnation or decline that often led to increasing per capita food supplies was quite likely associated with poverty in northeastern and mountainous central Japan but with ongoing (albeit vulnerable) protoindustrial prosperity in the cities of the Kantō and Kinki.

Adding our temporal data on natural disaster and rice prices, we might also offer speculative support for an improvement-and-sudden-reversal (or what Gurr [1970:53] would call "progressive deprivation") hypothesis: start with high pressure on the food supply, add gradual amelioration thereof, and then hit the country with a major crop failure, and increased conflict will be the result. Perhaps the pressure-breeds-conflict school, the resources-facilitate-conflict school, and the sudden-deprivation-stimulates-conflict school each has a grip on a different part of the phenomenon of collective action. An emerging consensus in the field suggests that popular contention results from self-conscious (although not necessarily formally "rational") balancing of interests (such as want or anger) and opportunities (provided by governmental vulnerability or resources in the hands of the people themselves). Our analysis has suggested that the likelihood of popular contention increases with interests—inferred from pressure on arable land and food supply—but also with opportunities—provided by movement away from bare subsistence. And the data on disasters and rice prices are consistent with both facets of the explanation: contention increases with sudden deprivation but actually peaks after the worst of the disasters and price spirals have passed, that is, when the adverse impact of both on governmental morale and control capabilities has finally sunk in.

What ties the whole together is the phenomenon of economic growth during the later Tokugawa period. Ordinarily one might expect a positive correlation between the curves visible in figures 2 (on natural disasters) and 4 (on rice prices) and between both of these curves and that seen in Figure 12 (on contention). But instead we see an inverse correlation between disasters and prices, and between disasters and conflict. We may conclude that the long-term rise in prices was not the result of poor harvests but the natural reflection of an economic upturn (exacerbated in the short run, at random moments, by disasters).[10] This protoindustry-driven upturn has been demonstrated elsewhere, as has its correlation with rising prices (Saitō 1985; Shimbo and Saitō 1989: 71). And the correlation between rice prices (see Figure 4) and contention is paralleled by significant positive correlations between contention and other price indices as well.[11]

The linkage between protoindustry-driven growth and conflict should come as no surprise: the former contributes to a larger vulnerable population (both rural and urban), to rising expectations, to new economic and potentially political resources in the hands of previously resource-poor groups, and also to secular price rises. The vulnerable population and rising expectations added to the inevitable climatically caused short-term reversals in a preindustrial economy contribute to higher levels of contention. The new resources contribute directly as well. And higher prices, when coupled with decreasing wages for the vulnerable urban population (a combination singularly acute during the Temmei and Tempō periods), create hardship that contributes quite plausibly to higher levels of contention.[12] Hence the results seen above: decreasing demographic pressure on the food supply covarying over the long run with increasing levels of popular contention, supplemented by short-term jumps in pressure (with price and wage consequences) that account for dramatic rises in levels of contention during periods of dearth. The package is not perfectly tied—the most vulnerable provinces and the phenomenon of political protest remain analytically opaque—but it suggests that in other spatial and behavioral spheres our exercise has been an instructive one.

Magnitude and Type of Conflict

The primary dependent variable used in this study is the magnitude of conflict, calculated both for different types of conflict and for the total amount of conflict occurring in each of the spatial units (631 counties or *gun*, 74 provinces or *kuni*, and 363 feudal domains or *han*) and temporal units (288 years) represented in the data. Thus two variables are needed: a typology of conflict events and a measure of the magnitude of each event. Such typologies are not hard to find (Kokushō 1971; Yokoyama 1977; Borton 1938; inter al.), but all of them are based either on the causes of conflict (e.g., Borton, Kokushō) or on the formal names of types of petitions, protests, village disputes, and riots—often legal terms with little relation to the magnitude of the events described. Measures of magnitude are rarer; to date only two quantitative studies of Edo-era protest have been made, and both weighted events according to the formal categories used by Aoki (Sugimoto 1978; Yokoyama 1977). These categories—which tend to be assigned according to the form of activity rather than its duration or intensity—cannot be ignored, since for many of the events in the Aoki *Nempyō*, supplementary data on the magnitude of conflict are missing. But because many events actually combine types of conflict (e.g., a village dispute followed by a petition, or a petition accompanied by a riot [see Sasaki 1973]), it is advisable to create a more elaborate typology and measure of magnitude.

Magnitude of Conflict

My first step was to code as many of the events in the Aoki *Nempyō* as possible according to Aoki's own categories. These categories and additional categorical descriptors appearing in the entry for each event were used, with a maximum of two descriptors per case. The result was 69 different types of events; 7370 of the total 7664 events in the *Nempyō* (96 percent) had at least one such descriptor assigned to them. This raw taxonomic resource far surpasses in detail the six to eight types of events used by Aoki and other historians to date. Some of these types, however, represented overlaps in judgment by coders and some represented the content of conflict (e.g., "tax strike") rather than its form; consequent combination of types reduced the number of types to 52.

The next step was to impose some theoretically meaningful order on the types derived from the *Nempyō*. Three intuitively important dimensions of conflict appear over and over in the literature on popular protest, or *ikki*: (a) whether a form of collective behavior is legal or illegal, (b) whether behavior is nonviolent or violent, and (c) whether conflict behavior is within the commoner class or directed at the warrior class or the formal institutions of government. These themes, somewhat elaborated, were adopted, and each of the 52 conflict types was categorized as

1. Legal or ambiguously legal (1)
   or
   Illegal (2);
2. Not violent/confrontational/challenging/challenging of the status quo, deferential (1)
   or Disorderly, challenging (by its very disorderliness), but weak or unfocused in its objectives, targets, and degree of dissatisfaction (2)
   or
   Aggressively, purposefully, actively, directly confrontational and challenging (3)
   or
   Violent toward persons and/or property (4);
3. Horizontal, among individuals or groups within the commoner class (1)
   or
   Vertical, between individuals or groups within the commoner class unequally situated in the socioeconomic or political hierarchy (2)
   or
   Vertical, between groups of commoners and the institutions or incumbents of the government (3).

The result of this categorization is the typology presented in Table A1.

My next step was to create three indices based on the three dimensions presented above and to see if these dimensions in fact bore any relationship to the empirical reality of the magnitude of the events so described. The coefficients presented in Table A2 indicate that, indeed, the dimensions theoretically derived above do bear substantial relation to this reality. The only surprise is that horizontal social conflict appears to be more aggressive and destructive than vertical political protest. Communal conflict may be smaller in scale but more intense, whereas political protest may be larger in scale but relatively deferential.

Given three empirically and theoretically meaningful dimensions of conflict, the next step is to reduce the 53 conflict types according to them. Therefore I created a new index in which each event was given a three-digit code in accordance with its values, for the first descriptor given for it, on the three dimensions of conflict. For example, an at-least-probably legal, politically nonchallenging, and horizontal intervillage border dispute would be coded 111 on this index, as suggested by columns 1 through 3 of Table A1. This index, as one may gather from the twelve groupings of event types in Table A1, has twelve categories (N.B. This is a categorical variable).

I then investigated whether or not these categories differ empirically, in two steps: First, I looked at the mean score of all events in each category on each of the six measures of conflict magnitude shown in Table A2. (To make sure that these groups were relatively homogeneous, especially on the horizontal-vertical dimension, I first examined the relative social position and political status of actors and target groups/individuals/institutions for each major type of event.) Since factor analysis of the six measures (see Table A2b) indicated two clear dimensions of conflict—scale or size (duration, number of participants, and number of villages involved) and aggressiveness (presence or absence of threatening or overtly aggressive behavior and number of structures destroyed or damaged)—the mean of the means of the events in each code category for each group of three magnitude measures was calculated and the two means were summed. The sums and the ranking of each category of conflict on a ten-point scale are presented in Table A3, columns 3 and 4. To corroborate this calculation and produce an interval measure of magnitude, the two factors emerging from the six measures of magnitude were also used to create two factor score-based variables, "aggressiveness" and "size." The mean score of each category of events on each of these two variables was calculated and the categories again ranked on a ten-point scale (see Table A3, columns 8 and 9). On each scale four natural groupings of the same categories appeared with only two slight within-group discrepancies, noted in column 9 (asterisked). The spacing of these clusters suggested the creation of a single new variable, "magnitude of conflict," with values of 1, 2, 5, and 10. Each of the 7370 typed events was therefore coded 1, 2, 5, or 10 based on the category in which its first descriptor placed it. If missing on the primary descriptor (that is, if the Aoki *Nempyō* did not formally classify it but described it with one of the accepted descriptors in the body of the entry for the event), then the secondary descriptor was used. For events that bore two descriptors, the larger (in magnitude) was used; thus, a communal conflict (*murakata sōdō*) that became a full-blown insurrection was coded as 10, not 1. The total conflict magnitude score for a given spatial or temporal unit, then, became the number of events of each type occurring in that unit multiplied by the magnitude of each event.

Types of Conflict

On the basis of the literature and an examination of the social, economic, and political relationships between actors and targets shown in the *Nempyō* data, the 62 types of conflict were divided into three categories—litigation and pleas ("litig."), social conflict ("soc."), and political protest ("polit.")—as shown in Table A1, column 5. If only one descriptor was given or if both descriptors were in the same category, the descriptor's category became the event's category. Combinations of descriptors were coded as shown in Figure A1, producing four types of conflict: litigation and petition, social conflict, political (or, more precisely perhaps, politicized social) conflict, and political protest. The "political conflict" category comprises events that (a) began as social conflict but resulted in recourse to political action not in the form of antigovernment protest but for

the purposes of seeking adjudication, restitution, compensation, or punishment or
that (b) consisted of litigation or petitioning the focus of which was some social
conflict. In the analyses presented here, magnitudes of conflict in each spatial or
temporal unit are calculated and analyzed for the totality of conflict and for each
of the four types of conflict.

Table A1
Categories of Conflict Events Based on Three Dimensions

1 Legal- Illegal	2 Deferential- Violent	3 Horizontal- Vertical	4	5
1	1	1	1. *Yoriai* (meeting)	Soc.
			2. *Murahachibu* (intravillage social ostracism)	Soc.
			3. *Kyōron* (village boundary disupte)	Soc.
			4. *Suiron* (dispute over water rights)	Soc.
			5. *Noron* (dispute over fields)	Soc.
			6. *Sanron* (dispute over village rights to mountain land and right to forest products)	Soc.
			7. *Gyoron* (dispute over fishing rights)	Soc.
			8. *Irefuda* (village election dispute)	Soc.
			9. *Zaron* (dispute concerning shrine-related village group)	Soc.
1	1	2	10. *Yōkyū* (unspecified request or demand)	Soc.
			11. *Funsō* (quarrel or dispute)	Soc.
			12. *Deiri* (quarrel or dispute)	Soc.
			13. *Murakata sōdō* (inter- or intra-village conflict)	Soc.
1	2	2	14. *Kosaku/hikan sōdō* (tenant dispute)	Soc.
			15. *Hyakushō sōdō* (dispute among or disorderly behavior by farmers)	Soc.
			16. *Fushinnin* (vote or decision of no confidence in village official[s])	Soc.
			17. *Kyūdan* (accusation of, e.g., village official malfeasance)	Soc.
			18. *Gishin* (expression of suspicion, accusation)	Soc.
1	1	3	19. *Shūso* (orderly petition or complaint)	Litig.

(*continued*)

(*Table A1, continued*))

1 Legal- Illegal	2 Deferential- Violent	3 Horizontal- Vertical	4	5
			20. *Hakoso* (petition placed in official petition box)	Litig.
			21. *Kuniso* (merchants' plea for commercial respite or advantage)	Litig.
1	1	3	22. *Soshō* (litigation)	Litig.
			23. *Negai* (plea, petition)	Litig.
			24. *Uttae* (plea, petition, litigation)	Litig.
1	2	3	25. *Fuon* (disorderly or contentious gathering)	Polit.
			26. *Tonshū* (disorderly or contentious gathering)	Polit.
			27. *Shōshū* (disorderly or contentious gathering)	Polit.
2	1	3	28. *Chikuden* (flight)	Polit.
			29. *Chōsan* (flight)	Polit.
			30. *Hariso* (complaint, plea, demand posted about or on wall or gate of relevant office)	Polit.
			31. *Suteso* (complaint, plea, demand scattered about the streets or before relevant office)	Polit.
			32. *Rempan* (circular, usually of signatures, demands, or action plans	Polit.
2	2	2	33. *Kome sōdō* (rice conflict or riot)	Soc.
			34. *Yonaoshi* (attack on rich merchants or farmers)	Soc.
			35. *Gōdan* (parley held under coercive conditions)	Soc.
			33. *Toshi sōjō* (urban conflict or riot)	Soc.
			37. *Sutoraiki* (labor strike)	Soc.
2	2	3	38. *Kagoso* (complaint, plea, demand presented to official in his palanquin)	Polit.
			39. *Jikiso* (complaint, etc., presented to official above official of first jurisdiction, "end run" appeal to higher office)	Polit.
			40. *Osso* (another term for "end run")	Polit.
			41. *Kadoso* (complaint, etc., left at gate of official's office or residence)	Polit.

(*continued*)

(*Table A1, continued*))

1 Legal- Illegal	2 Deferential- Violent	3 Horizontal- Vertical	4	5
			42. *Kakekomiso* (complaint, etc., lodged after entering office without permission)	Polit.
			43. *Rōjō* (shutting up or fortifying group in defiant position)	Polit.
			44. *Suwarikomi* (sit-in, sit-down strike)	Polit.
			45. *Totō* (conspiracy; gathering with apparently specific intent to protest)	Polit.
2	3	3	46. *Gōso* (complaint, etc., lodged aggressively, confrontationally, in defiance of proper procedures)	Polit.
2	4	2	47. *Uchikowashi* (destructive riot)	Polit.
2	4	3	48. *Sōran* (riot or insurrection)	Polit.
			49. *Hanran* (riot or insurrection)	Polit.
			50. *Dogō ikki* (insurrection)	Polit.
			51. *Buryoku tōsō* (armed insurrection)	Polit.
			52. *Hōki* (insurrection or rebellion)	Polit.

Table A2

(a) Correlations (Gammas) Between Three Dimensions of Conflict
   and Measures of Magnitude of Conflict

	Action is		
	Legal or Illegal	Deferential or Violent	Horizontal or Vertical
Action involves			
Threatening behavior	.78	.79	−.10 (n.s.)
Aggressive behavior	.83	.81	−.21
Destruction of			
buildings or property	.94	.86	−.71
Duration of event in days	.52	.56	.03 (n.s.)
Number of villages involved	.57	.57	.63
Number of participants	.67	.67	.30

N.s. = not statistically significant.

(b) Varimax Rotated Factor Analysis of Six Measures
   of Magnitude of Conflict

	Factor 1: Scale of Event	Factor 2: Aggressiveness
Action involves		
Threatening behavior	.09	.95
Aggressive behavior	.08	.95
Destruction	.20	.80
Duration of event	.68	.04
Number of villages involved	.85	.07
Number of participants	.80	.24

Table A3

Ranking of Event Categories in Terms of Measures of Conflict

Category of events (see Table A1)	1 Average of means of cases in category on three measures of aggressiveness of behavior	2 Average of means of cases in category on three measures of size of incident	3 Sum of averages	4 Sum of averages converted to 10-point scale	5 Summary magnitude score	6 Mean of cases in category on factore-score based measure of aggressive-ness behavior	7 Mean of cases in category on factor-score based measure of size of incident	8 Sum of means	9 Sum of means converted to 10-point scale	10 Summary magnitude score
1-2-2	-24	-52	-76	1.00		-23	-24	-47	1.22*	
1-1-2	-33.7	-31.3	-65	1.27		-34	-21	-55	1.00	
2-1-3	-32.7	-21.7	-54.4	1.54	1	-34	-12	-46	1.24	1
1-1-3	-39	-6	-45	1.75		-46	23	-23	1.86**	
2-2-3	-38	-5	-43	1.80		-44	18	-26	1.78**	
1-2-3	-9.3	-3.3	-12.6	2.53	2	-9	0	-9	2.24	2
2-3-3	14.3	47	61.3	4.33		13	41	54	3.94	
2-2-2	97.7	-21	76.7	4.72	5	110	-40	70	4.37	5
1-1-1	30	58.7	88.7	5.01		30	45	75	4.50	
2-4-2	226.7	65.3	292	9.95		239	35	274	9.87	
2-4-3	135.7	158.7	294.4	10.00	10	123	156	279	10.00	10

Primary descriptor indicates:

Secondary descriptor indicates:	litigation or legal plea	social conflict among commoners	remonstration or protest behavior
litigation or plea behavior	litigation/ petition	political conflict	political protest
social conflict among commoners	political conflict	social conflict	political protest
remonstration or protest behavior	political protest	political conflict	political protest

Figure A1. Qualitative classification of events in cases of multiple descriptors

Notes

Notes to Chapter One

1. Other aspects of population that deserve attention but are beyond the potential of the data used here include age and sex structure. I shall touch on each occasionally but attempt no systematic analysis.

2. There were in fact 74 provinces, but my data do not include Matsumae (presently Hokkaidō prefecture). When I speak of conflict per se here, I refer to the 73 provinces; when relating population to conflict, I have collapsed Mutsu, Rikuchū, Rikuzen, Iwashiro, and Iwaki provinces into Mutsu; and Ugo and Uzen provinces into Dewa; for a total of 68. Provinces are not ideal units of analysis. They are larger and fewer than Japan's 631 counties (*gun*). But county-level census data have not survived. Moreover, the provinces were not designed to vary on demographic or economic grounds; indeed, most were constituted as national microcosms: some highland, some lowland, some seacoast; some communications links; some cities, some countryside, and so forth. But in fact they vary considerably on the measures of interest here: e.g., frost-free days per year range from under 150 to more than 250; population varies from under 10,000 to over 1,000,000; and absolute agricultural productivity declined in some provinces while more than doubling in others.

3. Some of these analyses, of course, are not oversimple, but turn on the question of what is a significant relationship. Bohstedt (1983:11ff.), for example, finds correlations in the .30 to .40 range between food prices and riot behavior in eighteenth-century Britain and downplays them. Given imprecise data and the causal complexity of contentious behavior, it seems to me that these are substantial relationships indeed. Bohstedt rightly emphasizes community characteristics in calculating riot potential and causation (see also Calhoun 1982), but I would assert that the contribution of dearth is greater than he implies.

Notes to Chapter Two

1. The fourth, the Keiō famine of the late 1860s, occurred after the censuses ceased. The Kyōhō famine was most severe in the west, the Temmei and Tempō famines in the east.

2. The data on natural disasters used here are taken from Arakawa Hidetoshi's *Saigai no Rekishi* (1964:248–262). The Arakawa data are the only systematic compilation of such disasters for the period under examination, although probably not complete and in many instances quite imprecise (some events, for example, are given as affecting "eastern Japan" with no elaboration). Within these constraints, it is still possible to estimate the number of provinces affected by the events recorded (1108 during the years 1590–1877) if one does not insist on meretricious precision. For this analysis each province was recorded as being subject to a given disaster if it was specifically mentioned in Arakawa or if it was located in a region recorded as having been affected. Annual disaster figures were calculated as the number of provinces affected by all disasters recorded for each year (not the total number of disasters recorded, which was much lower). The annual data are given in this simple summed form; the provincial data were recoded into quartiles. This reduction of categories to four is costly in precision but, as mentioned, much of this precision is illusory given the crudity of Arakawa's original data. This presentation does indicate which provinces were relatively severely subject to the whims of nature and which ones were not. The types of disasters included by Arakawa in his compendium are wind and storm, flood, and rain damage to crops; excessive rain; drought; famine; epidemic; volcanic eruption; earthquake; and fire. They are not coded for intensity but for scope (number of provinces or regions affected) alone.

3. These data are taken from Iwahashi (1981). The composite scale is justified by the intercorrelations (r) of prices in the four cities, which range from .65 (Aizu and Hiroshima) to .94 (Ōsaka and Hiroshima).

4. One must recall here that the overwhelming bulk of government revenue came from the land tax; most nonagricultural pursuits were taxed lightly, if at all, despite accelerating official attempts to exploit them in the later Tokugawa period. Thus occupational exit from agriculture, even if not physical movement from the land, was the government's real concern.

5. Fifty thousand koku was roughly enough to feed 50,000 people for one year, or 600,000 people for one month, or more people if the period of relief were shorter than one month.

6. There was also an extraordinary amount of private litigation (Shigematsu 1986), but most of it did not overflow routine channels sufficiently to be included in Aoki's data.

7. The koku (approximately 5 bushels) was the standard measure of grain during the Tokugawa period, being the estimated amount necessary to feed one person for one year. It may be used as the surrogate for provincial population, since koku statistics are available for more units at more intervals and correlate with what population statistics are available at a consistent level of $r = c. 70$. In this case, the provincial assessment (*kokudaka*) for 1830 has been used (see Nakamura 1968:supplementary table 2).

8. The data shown in the maps may be summarized by means of correlation coefficients (r); the intercorrelations between the different dimensions of conflict (all statistically significant) are as follows:

	Social conflict	Political conflict	Political protest	Total conflict
Petition and litigation	.59	.52	.51	.65
Social conflict		.61	.34	.80
Political conflict			.38	.69
Political protest				.70

9. Agricultural vulnerability is a combination of mean provincial altitude and number of frost-free days per year; high vulnerability equals high altitude and few frost-free days (Geographical Survey Institute 1977; International Society 1974). Data on growth in agricultural productivity (land, labor, and total output) are from Nakamura 1968:175, 183. On protoindustrialization see Saitō 1985, and take special note of the extraordinary correspondence between the highly protoindustrial and highly contentious regions—central Japan, the Kinki, and the western Japan Sea coast—shown on p. 215 therein and in figures 7 through 10 in this volume.

10. The data on proportion of villages in the province governed directly by the bakufu are from Murakami 1983. Administrative fragmentation is calculated using number of feudal domains (Kodama 1979), Tokugawa bannermen or *hatamoto* domains (Suzuki 1962) and provincial area (Ōtomo 1979) in combination with proportion of the

province ruled by the bakufu; high fragmentation equals high proportion of bakufu villages and many feudal and *hatamoto* domains
with small average territories. See White 1988d.

11. With the sharp exception of Rikuzen, a province ruled almost in its
entirety by Sendai domain, which was noted for singularly effective
and consistent rule.

12. The data for this figure are, as before, "per-kokuized." The conflict
data for 1700–1740 are adjusted for provincial *kokudaka* in 1697;
those for 1825–1865, for the *kokudaka* in 1830 (Nakamura 1968).

13. The rice price data used here are those used in figures 4 and 5
above; the disaster data are from Arakawa 1964. Data on bakufu
financial situations are from Shimbo 1978; those on levels of bakufu
taxation are from Hara n.d.

14. Figure 13 is based on quinquennial totals of each type of conflict.

15. For fuller exposition of this topic in English and a rich bibliography
of Japanese sources, see Vlastos 1986; Kelly 1985; Walthall 1986;
Bix 1986. For the single best Japanese overview, see Aoki M. 1981,
especially the bibliography at the end of each volume.

16. I am speaking here of the difference between the average annual
magnitude of all forms of conflict during 1601–1625 compared to
the period 1676–1700.

17. In this light one should note the lack of correspondence between
population density (Saitō 1985:218) and figures 6 through 10
above.

18. This analysis, despite its crudity, confirms very closely the results I
found in an earlier exercise using different agricultural and conflict
data. The analysis is found in White 1981; the former data are from
Hanley and Yamamura 1977; the latter are from Yokoyama 1977.
The analysis is further corroborated by simple correlation of
changes in agricultural productivity with conflict. Two different
measures of productivity increase (Nakamura 1968:175, 183) correlate with our four types of conflict and their total at between $-.13$
and $-.27$.

19. Perhaps this is why diminishing pressure on the food supply co-
exists with agricultural vulnerability as a correlate of conflict: vulnerability is related to all four types of conflict and to total magnitude at between $r = .26$ and $r = .38$.

20. Perhaps this explains the direct relationship between conflict and
the price of rice: the four-city mean annual price (see Figure 4) is
correlated with all the forms of conflict, except petition and litigation, as well as with the total magnitude of conflict at between
$r = .34$ and $r = .43$.

Notes to Chapter Three

1. Eighteenth-century provincial population is the average of provincial populations in 1750, 1756, and 1786, as taken from Hayami Akira's revision of the bakufu survey data (xerox, n.d.). For the nineteenth century, the data for 1822, 1828, and 1834 were averaged. Where one of these three pieces of data was missing or questionable, the other two were averaged. Growth or decline in the eighteenth century was the percentage change in population size between the 1721 and 1798 surveys; that in the nineteenth was the percentage change between 1798 and 1846.

2. In calculating these measures, the figures for both population size and change (see note 1) were divided by province area data taken from Ōtomo (1979:24–26) or arable land area (in *chō*; 1 *chō* = 2.45 acres) taken from the 1875 *Kyōbu Seihyō* (Rikugun 1976), recoded into quartiles to compensate for possible changes during the era.

3. Population data for these measures are those described in note 1. For eighteenth-century productivity the provincial *kokudaka* in 1697 was used; for the nineteenth century the *kokudaka* for 1830 was used (Nakamura 1968). In all instances the resulting figures were divided into quartiles. For taxes provincial tax rates in 1872 were taken from Nakamura (1968) and recoded into quartiles; net *kokudaka* per capita was gross *kokudaka* per capita less the share taken by the provincial tax rate. I could not compute measures of change in *kokudaka* per capita for each century, because the only *kokudaka* figures available were for 1697 and 1830; thus only a single measure of change was calculated, and it was correlated with aggregate measures of conflict of each type in both the eighteenth and nineteenth centuries added together.

4. Data on calories per capita were calculated from the total provincial production of edible agricultural products (*futsū nōsambutsu*) in the 1870s, as shown in Fujiwara 1964, recoded into quartiles. Net calories were calculated from the same tax data used in note 20 of Chapter 2.

5. Two measures of change in agricultural productivity were used, both using data from Nakamura 1968. The first measured change in agricultural output between 1700 and 1880; the second measured change in both labor and land productivity between 1720 and 1880; both were dichotomized. Measures of population pressure were calculated by combining these data with dichotomized population data for the entire era, creating two four-point scales

running from (a) decreasing or minimally increasing population combined with maximum growth in productivity at one extreme to (b) maximum population increase combined with minimally increasing productivity at the other.

6. The data are taken from Rikugun 1976. The proportion of population in each province living in settlements of 3000 or more in 1875 was used, recoded into quartiles.

7. The four factors were unweighted because their intercorrelations were all in the range of $r = .30$ to .40, with the exception of urbanism, whose intercorrelations averaged .18. But urbanism is a three-point scale, whereas the others are four-point scales, so the original scales were multiplied without creating standardized scores.

8. The merely suggestive nature of the results is also imposed by the nature of the data: I will be subdividing our 70-odd provinces into smaller groups, often of no more than 20. With eight independent variables and few cases, the results of such a regression are unstable. I ran the analysis using different methods of data input; both the significance levels of the results and the results of the SPSS computer program's multicollinearity diagnostic routine (Norusis 1985; SPSS 1983) indicate that we are on fairly firm ice. Still, caution is called for.

9. As noted above, the bakufu censuses undercounted significant numbers of people. Additionally, certain domains did not include small children. Saitō Osamu (1988) specifies eleven provinces in which the predominant domains excluded children. Of these, only eight excluded significant groups, but even the presumption of such error does not move these provinces into higher size categories. Were it to do so, the relationship between size and conflict would become even weaker, since six of the eight were below the mean conflict level already.

10. I am indebted to Saitō Osamu for several of the following strands of thought.

11. I have examined three such indices: a composite index of retail prices in Kyōto, a consumer price index from Kyōto, and an index of wholesale prices in Ōsaka (Umemura 1961:175; Shimbo 1978:30ff.; Saitō 1975:772); their relationships to the four types of contention ranged between $r = .22$ and .50, .20 and .44, and .21 and .47, respectively. Granted, these indices are local; still, the Kinai region to which they pertain was the locomotive for the entire national economy. Presumably they predict even more powerfully contention in the Kinai region than in the nation as a whole.

12. A measure of wages in the Kyōto building trades (Umemura 1961:175) correlates at approximately −.50 with all three of the price indices discussed in note 11 and at between −.14 and −.41 with our measures of conflict.

References

Aoki Kōji. 1966. *Hyakushō Ikki no Nenjiteki Kenkyū.* Tokyo.

————. 1981. *Hyakushō Ikki Sōgō Nempyō.* Tokyo.

Aoki Michio et al. 1981. *Ikki.* Tokyo.

Arakawa Hidetoshi. 1964. *Saigai no Rekishi.* Tokyo.

————. 1967. *Kikin no Rekishi.* Tokyo.

Barnes, Samuel, Max Kaase, et al. 1979. *Political Action.* Beverly Hills.

Beasley, William. 1967. *The Modern History of Japan.* New York.

Bird, Isabella. 1880. *Unbeaten Tracks in Japan.* 2 vols. New York.

Bix, Herbert. 1986. *Peasant Protest in Japan, 1590–1884.* New Haven.

Bohstedt, John. 1983. *Riots and Community Politics in England and Wales.* Cambridge.

Borton, Hugh. 1938. "Peasant Uprisings in Japan of the Tokugawa Period." *Transactions of the Asia Society of Japan,* second series, vol. 16, May, p. 1.

Bowen, Roger. 1988. "Japanese Peasants: Moral? Rational? Revolutionary? Duped?" *Journal of Asian Studies,* vol. 47, no. 4 (November), p. 821.

Brinton, Crane. 1965. *The Anatomy of Revolution.* New York.

Calhoun, Craig. 1982. *The Question of Class Struggle.* Chicago.

Chevalier, Louis. 1958. *Classes laborieuses et classes dangereuses à Paris pendant la première moitié du XIXe siècle.* Paris.

Choucri, Nazli. 1974. *Population Dynamics and International Violence.* Lexington.

Choucri, Nazli, ed. 1984. *Multidisciplinary Perspectives on Population and Conflict.* Syracuse.

Cornelius, Wayne. 1970. "The Political Sociology of Cityward Migration in Latin America." In Francine Rabinowitz and Felicity Trueblood, eds., *Latin American Urban Annual.* Beverly Hills.

————. 1975. *Politics and the Urban Poor in Mexico City.* Stanford.

Dahl, Robert, and Edward Tufte. 1973. *Size and Democracy.* Stanford.

Davies, James, ed. 1971. *When Men Revolt and Why.* New York.

DeNardo, James. 1985. *Power in Numbers.* Princeton.

Fruin, Mark. 1973. "Farm Family Migration: The Case of Echizen in the Nineteenth Century." *Keiō Economic Studies,* vol. 10, no. 2, p. 37.

Fujioka Kenjirō. 1966. *Nihon Rekishi Chiri Handobukku.* Tokyo.

Fujiwara Masato. 1964. *Meiji Zenki Sangyō Hattatsu Shi Shiryō.* Bessatsu 1–5. Tokyo.

Fukaya Katsumi. 1979. *Hyakushō Ikki no Rekishiteki Kōzō.* Tokyo.

Geographical Survey Institute. 1977. *National Atlas of Japan.* Tokyo.

Goldstone, Jack. 1988. "East and West in the Seventeenth Century: Political Crises in Stuart England, Ottoman Turkey, and Ming China." *Comparative Studies in Sociology and History, vol. 30, no. 1, p. 103.*

––––––. n.d. "The Origins of the English Revolution." Unpublished ms., Northwestern University.

Greenough, Paul. 1983. "Indulgence and Abundance as Asian Peasant Values." *Journal of Asian Studies,* vol. 42, no. 4 (August), p. 831.

Gurr, Ted. 1968. "A Causal Model of Civil Strife." *American Political Science Review,* vol. 62, no. 4 (December), p. 1104.

––––––. 1970. *Why Men Rebel.* Princeton.

Gurr, Ted, ed. 1980. *Handbook of Political Conflict.* New York.

Gurr, Ted, and Herman Weil. 1973. "Population Growth and Political Conflict." Unpublished ms., Northwestern University.

Hall, John, and Marius Jansen, eds. 1968. *Studies in the Institutional History of Early Modern Japan.* Princeton.

Hanley, Susan. 1973. "Migration and Economic Change in Okayama during the Tokugawa Period." *Keiō Economic Studies,* vol. 10, no. 2, p. 19.

Hanley, Susan, and Kozo Yamamura. 1977. *Economic and Demographic Change in Preindustrial Japan, 1600–1868.* Princeton.

Hara Akira. n.d. "Bakuhan-sei Shakai no Gaikan." Unpublished data.

Harada Tomohiko. 1982. *Kinsei Toshi Sōjō Shi.* Kyoto.

Hayami, Akira. 1973a. "Labor Migration in a Pre-Industrial Society." *Keiō Economic Studies,* vol. 10, no. 2, p. 1.

––––––. 1973b. *Kinsei Nōson no Rekishi Jinkōgakuteki Kenkyū.* Tokyo.

––––––. 1975. "Kinsei Kōki Chiiki-betsu Jinkō Hendō to Toshi Jinkō Hiritsu no Kanren." *Tokugawa Rinseishi Kenkyū-jo Kenkyū Kiyō,* no. 9, p. 230.

––––––. 1978. "Nōbi Chihō no Rekishi Jinkōgakuteki Kenkyū Josetsu." *Tokugawa Rinseishi Kenkyū-jo Kenkyū Kiyō,* no. 12, p. 197.

––––––. 1982a. "Kinsei Ōu Chihō Jinkō no Shiteki Kenkyū Joron." *Mita Gakkai Zasshi,* vol. 75 no. 3 (June), p. 70.

––––––. 1982b. "A 'Great Transformation.'" Paper presented to the Third International Studies Conference on Japan, The Hague, September.

––––––. 1988. *Edo no Nōmin Seikatsu Shi.* Tokyo.

Hayashi Motoi. 1976. *Zoku Hyakushō Ikki no Dentō.* Tokyo.

Hibbs, Douglas. 1973. *Mass Political Violence.* New York.

Honjo, Eijiro. 1935. *The Social and Economic History of Japan.* Kyoto.

Huntington, Samuel. 1968. *Political Order in Changing Societies.* New Haven.

Hyakushō Ikki Kenkyū Kai, ed. 1980. *Tempō-ki no Jimmin Tōsō to Shakai Henkaku.* Vol. 2. Tokyo.

Iida Bunya. 1976. "Kōfu Han." In Kodama Kōta, ed., *Shimpen Monogatari Hanshi,* vol. 4. Tokyo.

_____. 1979. "Tempō Jusannen 'Kōfu Kami-fuchū Kyūmin Gōkyū Sangyōshiki' to sono Haikei." *Shinano,* vol. 31, no. 6 (June 1), p. 10.

International Society for Educational Information. 1974. *Atlas of Japan.* Tokyo.

Iwahashi Masaru. 1981. *Kinsei Nihon Bukka Shi no Kenkyū.* Tokyo.

Jannetta, Ann. 1987. *Epidemics and Mortality in Early Modern Japan.* Princeton.

Jansen, Marius, and Gilbert Rozman. 1986. *Japan in Transition.* Princeton.

Kajinishi Mitsuhaya. 1978. *Chiso Kaisei to Chihō Jichi Sei.* Meiji Shi Kenkyū Sōsho, vol. 2. Tokyo.

Kelly, William. 1985. *Deference and Defiance in Nineteenth-Century Japan.* Princeton.

Kishimoto Minoru. 1961. *Awa ni okeru Nōmin Rison no Chirigakuteki Kenkyū.* Tokushima.

Kitajima Masamoto. 1966. *Bakuhansei no Kumon.* Tokyo.

Kitō Hiroshi. 1983a. "Edo Jidai no Beishoku." *Rekishigaku Kōron,* April.

_____. 1983b. *Nihon Nisennen no Jinkō Shi.* Kyoto.

_____. 1985. "Seijuku Shakai no Jinkō." *Sekai to Jinkō,* June, p. 60.

Kodama Kōta. 1979. *Hanshi Sōran.* Tokyo.

Kōfu Machi Bugyō. N.d. *Goyō Nikki.* Personal communication from Iida Bunya, July 1979.

Kōfu Machikata Kasū Ninzu no Shirabe-sho. 1870. Kōfu, September.

Kōfu Ryakushi. 1918. Kōfu.

Kojima Shigeyuki. 1979. "Umemura Sōdō no Kisoteki Kenkyū." *Shinano,* vol. 31 no. 6 (June 1), p. 50.

Kokushō Iwao. 1971. *Hyakushō Ikki no Kenkyū, Zokuhen.* Tokyo.

Kuhn, Philip. 1970. *Rebellion and Its Enemies in Late Imperial China.* Cambridge.

Masaoka, Kanji et al. 1988. "Timing of Role Transitions and the Life Course of Japanese Peasants." Paper presented at the Nōbi Regional Project workshop, Nagoya, January.

McClintock, Cynthia. 1987. "Peru's Sendero Luminoso Rebellion: Origins and Trajectory." Unpublished ms., George Washington University.

Mendels, Franklin. 1982. "Proto-Industrialization: Theory and Reality." In International Economic History Association, ed., *Eighth International Economic History Congress, Budapest 1982, "A" Themes*, p. 69. Budapest, Akademiai Kiado.

Midlarsky, Manus. 1982. "Scarcity and Inequality." *Journal of Conflict Resolution*, vol. 26, no. 1 (March), p. 3.

Minami Kazuo. 1978. *Bakumatsu Edo Shakai no Kenkyū*. Tokyo.

Miyamoto Matarō and Kozo Yamamura. 1981. "Ryō-Taisenkanki Kosaku Sōgi no Sūryō Bunseki e no Isshikiron." In Nakamura Takafusa, ed., *Senkanki no Nihon Keizai Bunseki*, p. 389. Tokyo.

Moore, Barrington. 1978. *Injustice*. White Plains, N.Y.

Mosk, Carl, and Simon Pak. 1977. "Food Consumption, Physical Characteristics, and Population Growth in Japan, 1874–1940." Working paper 102, Center for Japanese and Korean Studies, University of California, Berkeley.

Muller, Edward. 1979. *Aggressive Political Participation*. Princeton.

Murakami Tadashi. 1983. "Edo Bakufu Chokkatsuryō no Chiikiteki Bumpu ni tsuite." *Hōsei Shigaku*, no. 25 (February), p. 1.

Murdock, M. R. 1987. "Letters to the Editor." *Chapel Hill Newspaper*, April 23.

Nagasu Toshiyuki. 1986. *Osso*. Tokyo.

Najita, Tetsuo, and Victor Koschmann, eds. 1982. *Conflict in Modern Japanese History*. Princeton.

Nakamura Satoru. 1968. *Meiji Ishin no Kiso Kōzō*. Tokyo.

Nishikawa Shunsaku. 1979. *Edo Jidai no Poritikaru Ekonomii*. Tokyo.

———. 1985. *Nihon Keizai no Seichō Shi*. Tokyo.

Norusis, Marija. 1985. *SPSS-X Advanced Statistics Guide*. New York.

Oberschall, Anthony. 1973. *Social Conflict and Social Movements*. Englewood·Cliffs, N.J.

Ōkawa Kazushi, ed. 1976. *Chōki Keizai Tokei*. Vol. 6. Tokyo.

Ōtomo Atsushi. 1979. *Nihon Toshi Jinkō Bumpu Ron*. Tokyo.

Ōuchi Tsutomu. 1980. *Nihon ni okeru Nōminsō no Bunkai*. Tokyo.

Parvin, Manoucher. 1973. "Economic Determinants of Political Unrest." *Journal of Conflict Resolution*, vol. 17, no. 2 (June), p. 271.

Perry, Elizabeth. 1980. *Rebels and Revolutionaries in North China, 1845–1945*. Stanford.

Rekishigaku Kenkyū Kai et al., eds. 1985. *Kōza Nihon Shi*. Vol. 6. Tokyo.

Rikugun Sambō-bu, ed. 1976. *Kyōbu Seihyō.* Tokyo.

Saitō Osamu. 1975. "Ōsaka Oroshi-uri Bukka Shisū, 1757–1915-nen." *Mita Gakkai Zasshi,* vol. 68, no. 10, p. 769.

———. 1985. *Puroto-Kōgyōka no Jidai.* Tokyo.

———. 1986. "Changing Structure of Urban Employment and Its Effects on Migration Patterns in 18th and 19th Century Japan." Discussion paper no. 134, Institute of Economic Research, Hitotsubashi University, March.

———. 1988. "Jinkō Hendō ni okeru Nishi to Higashi." In Odaka Kōnosuke and Yamamoto Yūzō, eds., *Bakumatsu-Meiji no Nihon Keizai,* p. 29. Tokyo.

Sanders, David. 1981. *Patterns of Political Instability.* New York.

Sasaki Junnosuke. 1973. *Murakata Sōdō to Yonaoshi.* Vol. 2. Tokyo.

———. 1979. *Yonaoshi.* Tokyo.

Sasaki Junnosuke, ed. 1974. *Hyakushō Ikki to Uchikowashi.* Tokyo.

Sasaki Yoichirō. 1966. "Tokugawa Jidai Kōki Toshi Jinkō no Kenkyū."

———. 1969. "Hida-no-kuni Takayama no Jinkō Kenkyū." In Shakai Keizai Shigakkai, ed., *Keizai shi ni okeru jinkō,* p. 95. Tokyo.

———. 1978. "Migration and Fertility in Tokugawa Japan." Paper presented at the Conference on Historical Demography and Family History in East Asia, Oxford University, August.

Scheiner, Irwin. 1973. "The Mindful Peasant." *Journal of Asian Studies,* vol. 32, no. 4 (August), p. 579.

Scott, James. 1976. *The Moral Economy of the Peasant.* New Haven.

Sekiyama Naotarō. 1948. *Kinsei Nihon Jinkō no Kenkyū.* Tokyo.

———. 1958. *Kinsei Nihon no Jinkō Kōzō.* Tokyo.

———. 1959. *Nihon no Jinkō.* Tokyo.

Shigematsu Kazuyoshi. 1986. *Edo no Hanzai Hakusho.* Tokyo.

Shimbo Hiroshi. 1978. *Kinsei no Bukka to Keizai Hatten.* Tokyo.

Shimbo Hiroshi and Saitō Osamu, eds. 1989. *Kindai Seichō no Taidō.* Tokyo.

Shingles, Richard. 1987. "Relative Deprivation and the Inclination to Protest." Unpublished ms., Virginia Polytechnic Institute, March.

Skinner, William. 1979. "Social Ecology and the Forces of Repression in North China." Paper presented at the ACLS Workshop on Rebellion and Revolution in North China, Harvard University, July.

———. 1987. "The Historical Geography of Population Processes in China, Japan, and France." Paper presented at the Social Science History Seminar, Miami University, April.

Smith, Henry. 1981. "From Edo to Tokyo: The Provincial Interlude." Paper prepared for the Tokugawa–Meiji Transition Workshop, Lake Wilderness, Washington.

Smith, Thomas. 1959. *The Agrarian Origins of Modern Japan*. Stanford.

———. 1977. *Nakahara*. Stanford.

SPSS Inc. 1983. *SPSS-X Users' Guide*. New York.

Sugimoto, Yoshio. 1975. "Structural Sources of Popular Revolts and the Tobaku Movement at the Time of the Meiji Restoration." *Journal of Asian Studies*, vol. 34, no. 4 (August), p. 875.

———. 1978. "Peasant Rebellion and Ruling Class Adaptation at the Time of the Meiji Restoration in Japan." Paper presented at the World Congress of Sociology, Uppsala, August.

Suzuki Hisashi. 1962. "Tokugawa Bakushindan no Chigyō Keitai." *Shigaku Zasshi*, vol. 71, no. 2, p. 1.

Taeuber, Irene. 1958. *The Population of Japan*. Princeton.

Tilly, Charles. 1968. "Collective Violence in Nineteenth Century French Cities." Paper presented at Reed College, February.

———. 1978. *From Mobilization to Revolution*. Reading.

———. 1982. "Proletarianization and Rural Collective Action in East Anglia and Elsewhere, 1500–1900." *Journal of Peasant Studies*, vol. 10, Fall, p. 5.

Tilly, Charles, et al. 1975. *The Rebellious Century*. Cambridge.

Tōkyō Hyakunen Shi Henshū Iinkai, ed. 1973. *Tōkyō Hyakunen Shi*. Vols. 1, 2. Tokyo.

Tōkyō-fu. 1935. *Tōkyō-fu Shi*. Vol. 1. Tokyo.

Tong, James. 1985. "Rebellions and Banditry in the Ming Dynasty (1368–1644): A Rational-Choice Model." Paper presented at the annual meeting of the American Political Science Association, New Orleans, August.

Toyoda Takeshi. 1962. *Nihon no Hōken Toshi*. Tokyo.

Tsuda Hideo. 1970. *Hōken Shakai Kaitai Katei Kenkyū Josetsu*. Tokyo.

———. 1977. *Bakumatsu Shakai no Kenkyū*. Tokyo.

Tsuda Ryōichi. 1978. "Kinsei Kōfu Jōkamachi ni okeru Toshi Kōzō no Henyō Katei." *Rekishi Chirigaku Kiyō*, no. 20, p. 179.

Umemura Mataji. 1961. "Kenchikugyō Rōdōsha no Jisshitsu Chingin, 1726–1958." *Keizai Kenkyū*, vol. 12, no. 2 (April), p. 172.

———. 1965. "Tokugawa Jidai no Jinkō Sūsei to sono Kisei Yōin." *Keizai Kenkyū*, vol. 16, no. 2 (April), p. 133.

Vlastos, Stephen. 1986. *Peasant Protests and Uprisings in Tokugawa Japan*. Berkeley.

Walthall, Anne. 1986. *Social Protest and Popular Culture in Eighteenth-Century Japan*. Tucson.

White, James. 1973. *Political Implications of Cityward Migration: Japan as an Exploratory Test Case*. Beverly Hills.

————. 1981. "Population Movement and Sociopolitical Change During the Tokugawa–Meiji Transition." Paper presented at the Tokugawa–Meiji Transition Workshop, Lake Wilderness, Washington, August.

————. 1988a. "Social Conflict and Political Protest in the Nōbi Region, 1590–1877." Paper presented at the Nōbi Regional Project Workshop, Nagoya, January.

————. 1988b. "The Rational Rioters: Leaders, Followers, and Popular Protest in Early Modern Japan." *Politics and Society,* vol. 16, no. 1 (March), p. 35.

————. 1988c. "State Growth and Popular Protest in Tokugawa Japan." *Journal of Japanese Studies,* vol. 14, no. 1 (Winter), p. 1.

————. 1988d. "State Control and Sociopolitical Conflict in Japan, 1600–1868." Paper prepared for the annual meeting of the American Political Science Association, Sept.

————. 1989. "Economic Development and Sociopolitical Unrest in Nineteenth-Century Japan." *Economic Development and Cultural Change,* vol. 37, no. 2 (January), p. 231.

White, James, ed. 1979. *The Urban Impact of Internal Migration.* Chapel Hill.

Wolf, Eric. 1969. *Peasant Wars of the Twentieth Century.* New York.

Yamada Tadao. 1984. *Ikki Uchikowashi no Undō Kōzō.* Tokyo.

Yokoyama Toshio. 1977. *Hyakushō Ikki to Gimin Denshō.* Tokyo.

Yomiuri Shimbun Sha, ed. 1967. *Tōkyō no Hyakunen.* Vol. 1. Tokyo.

Yunoki Jūzō and Horie Yasuzō. 1930. "Hompō Jinkō Hyō." *Keizai Shi Kenkyū,* p. 188.

Zimmermann, Ekkart. 1983. *Political Violence, Crises, and Revolutions.* Cambridge, Mass.

CHINA RESEARCH MONOGRAPHS (CRM)

6. David D. Barrett. *Dixie Mission: The United States Army Observer Group in Yenan, 1944,* 1970 ($4.00)
17. Frederic Wakeman, Jr., Editor. *Ming and Qing Historical Studies in the People's Republic of China,* 1981 ($10.00)
21. James H. Cole. *The People Versus the Taipings: Bao Lisheng's "Righteous Army of Dongan,"* 1981 ($7.00)
24. Pao-min Chang. *Beijing, Hanoi, and the Overseas Chinese,* 1982 ($7.00)
25. Rudolf G. Wagner. *Reenacting the Heavenly Vision: The Role of Religion in the Taiping Rebellion,* 1984 ($12.00)
27. John N. Hart. *The Making of an Army "Old China Hand": A Memoir of Colonel David D. Barrett,* 1985 ($12.00)
28. Steven A. Leibo. *Transferring Technology to China: Prosper Giquel and the Self-strengthening Movement,* 1985 ($15.00)
29. David Bachman. *Chen Yun and the Chinese Political System,* 1985 ($15.00)
30. Maria Hsia Chang. *The Chinese Blue Shirt Society: Fascism and Developmental Nationalism,* 1985 ($15.00)
31. Robert Y. Eng. *Economic Imperialism in China: Silk Production and Exports, 1861–1932,* 1986 ($15.00)
33. Yue Daiyun. *Intellectuals in Chinese Fiction,* 1988 ($10.00)
34. Constance Squires Meaney. *Stability and the Industrial Elite in China and the Soviet Union,* 1988 ($15.00)
35. Yitzhak Shichor. *East Wind over Arabia: Origins and Implications of the Sino-Saudi Missile Deal,* 1989 ($7.00)
36. Suzanne Pepper. *China's Education Reform in the 1980s: Policies, Issues, and Historical Perspectives,* 1990 ($12.00)
37. Joyce K. Kallgren, Editor. *Building a Nation-State: China after Forty Years,* 1990 ($12.00)
sp. Phyllis Wang and Donald A. Gibbs, Editors. *Readers' Guide to China's Literary Gazette, 1949–1979,* 1990 ($20.00)
38. James C. Shih. *Chinese Rural Society in Transition: A Case Study of the Lake Tai Area, 1368–1800,* 1992 ($15.00)
39. Anne Gilks. *The Breakdown of the Sino-Vietnamese Alliance, 1970–1979,* 1992 ($15.00)
sp. Theodore Han and John Li. *Tiananmen Square Spring 1989: A Chronology of the Chinese Democracy Movement,* 1992 ($10.00)
40. Frederic Wakeman, Jr., and Wen-hsin Yeh, Editors. *Shanghai Sojourners,* 1992 ($20.00)

KOREA RESEARCH MONOGRAPHS (KRM)

7. Quee-Young Kim. *The Fall of Syngman Rhee,* 1983 ($12.00)
9. Helen Hardacre. *The Religion of Japan's Korean Minority: The Preservation of Ethnic Identity,* 1985 ($12.00)
10. Fred C. Bohm and Robert R. Swartout, Jr., Editors. *Naval Surgeon in Yi Korea: The Journal of George W. Woods,* 1984 ($12.00)
11. Robert A. Scalapino and Hongkoo Lee, Editors. *North Korea in a Regional and Global Context,* 1986 ($20.00)
13. Vipan Chandra. *Imperialism, Resistance, and Reform in Late Nineteenth-Century Korea: Enlightenment and the Independence Club,* 1988 ($17.00)
14. Seok Choong Song. *Explorations in Korean Syntax and Semantics,* 1988 ($20.00)
15. Robert A. Scalapino and Dalchoong Kim, Editors. *Asian Communism: Continuity and Transition,* 1988 ($20.00)
16. Chong-Sik Lee and Se-Hee Yoo, Editors. *North Korea in Transition,* 1991 ($12.00)
17. Nicholas Eberstadt and Judith Banister. *The Population of North Korea,* 1992 ($12.00)

JAPAN RESEARCH MONOGRAPHS (JRM)

7. Teruo Gotoda. *The Local Politics of Kyoto,* 1985 ($15.00)
8. Yung H. Park. *Bureaucrats and Ministers in Contemporary Japanese Government,* 1986 ($15.00)